P9-DES-275

"Melody Rossi ... ... unity a compassionate, comprehensive, insightful, ... helpful guide to the spiritual care of the dying. . . . Her emphasis upon servanthood is both spiritual and highly effective."
—**Frederick E. Goos**, DMin, PhD, LMFT
Bereavement Coordinator,
South Jersey Healthcare
Hospice Care

"*May I Walk You Home?* is a very thoughtful, practical, and easy-to-read book. It offers wonderful insights and suggestions for the spiritual, emotional, and practical problems that surround the dying of a loved one. As a physician and a Christian, I think this book would be an extraordinarily useful guide for family and friends of patients who are facing a terminal illness."
—**Nancy B. Edwards**, MD
Associate Professor of Clinical Pediatrics,
USC Keck School of Medicine

"As a Christian healthcare worker—cautioned in my earlier years of training not to impose my own spiritual beliefs on patients—I have sometimes felt trapped between the tenets of my profession and the call to reflect Christ's love in my work. Melody Rossi helps us, as caregivers, to see how God can equip us to minister to patients and loved ones in His special way—not only in addressing physical needs but also in offering God's message of hope, peace, and love."
—**Marilyn K. Eisz**, RN, MN
Healthcare Leader, Educator, and Consultant

"All of us at some time are going to experience grief over a loved one who is dying. . . . Melody's real-life stories will help you walk through the process of a loved one going Home, as well as show you how to prepare them for the journey."
—**Kathleen Jackson**
Speaker, Author, and Founder of the
Godly Business Woman Magazine

May I Walk You Home?

MELODY ROSSI

BETHANYHOUSE
Minneapolis, Minnesota

Published by Bethany House Publishers
11400 Hampshire Avenue South
Bloomington, Minnesota 55438

Bethany House Publishers is a division of
Baker Publishing Group, Grand Rapids, Michigan.

Printed in the United States of America

ISBN-13:   978-0-7642-0355-8
ISBN-10:   0-7642-0355-X

Library of Congress Cataloging-in-Publication Data
Rossi, Melody.
     May I walk you home? : sharing Christ's love with the dying / Melody Rossi.
          p.   cm.
     Summary: "Presents information on how to discuss spiritual matters with someone who is terminally ill. Addresses end-of-life issues, including physical and emotional aspects, as well as grief and loss"—Provided by publisher.
     ISBN-13: 978-0-7642-0355-8 (pbk.)
     ISBN-10: 0-7642-0355-X (pbk.)
     1. Church work with the terminally ill.   2. Terminally ill—Religious life.
3. Death—Religious aspects—Christianity.   I. Title.
     BV4460.6.R67   2007
     259'.4175—dc22   2006038407

To Jan Ladd and Vernie Pritchett
By walking alongside me, you led me to Jesus.

And to Pride
You are my love. You are my song.

ACKNOWLEDGMENTS

The journey that resulted in this book was a long one, and represents a group effort. My heart is filled with gratitude for all those who made significant contributions along the way.

To Marita, Florence, and Lauren Littauer and all my friends at CLASS (Christian Leaders, Authors, and Speakers Services), thank you for teaching me the nuts and bolts of writing and speaking. You are the most generous of mentors.

Jennifer Trost and Doug and Michele Boyer, your gift of a quiet place to write was an essential component of this effort. I couldn't have managed without the solitude. Sherri Browning, Patti Pedrick, John Wetzel, Art and Jan Rennels, thank you for reading and editing my manuscript and for your invaluable comments and corrections. I know it was a labor of love. Kelly Montgomery, for cheerfully reading every word of *every* version, and dreaming with me about this book long before anything was ever put to paper, I salute you. You deserve a special place in the Friendship Hall of Fame for your cheerleading efforts.

Gary Johnson and Kyle Duncan, thank you for understanding the message of this book and for your commitment to ministry in publishing. The entire Bethany House family has given me the warmest of welcomes, but I would especially like to commend Julie Smith, Tim Peterson, Linda White, Brett Benson, and Eric Walljasper for the creativity and expertise you have leant to this project. Jeff Braun, you are a true blessing. Your editorial suggestions and wise insights have been invaluable and your hand-holding and gentle spirit are greatly appreciated. Thank you for asking me to think through issues I overlooked and for your careful attention to every detail. This book is immensely better because of you.

Bill Jensen, my opera buddy, agent, and treasured friend,

thank you for your unwavering encouragement, for shedding a tear over my stories, and for helping me find my voice. You have been my champion, and this book would never have been written without you. Mille grazie.

Kelly and Emma, for keeping Cloud and Fire Ministries running smoothly while I was writing, may God repay you at least ten-fold. Both of you are rare and beautiful gems and amazing co-laborers in Christ.

Carole "Barnabus" Walker, your constancy in friendship and prayer sustained me so I could tend to the needs of others. The battles you waged in the heavenly realm have availed much.

For the friends who walked alongside me in countless ways while my parents were dying, I am deeply grateful. Whether you worked on my mother's house, came to the hospital, or performed other acts of kindness in Jesus' name, I hope you know that your contribution was deeply significant to my parents and to me. Special thanks to Eula, Marvin, Vernie, Al, Sam, Betty, Rick, Kelly, Robin, Nita, Jeff, Sherri, Juan, Ryan, Kevin, John, Marilyn, the MPC deacons and CFM kids, and the many others who did so much. Together, we brought in this harvest.

Thank you, Patti, for sharing your mother with me. I loved her.

Stan and Kristy, both of you are incredible. You went beyond the call of duty with Mom, but were absolutely amazing with Dad. I am proud to call you family.

There are no words to express the respect and admiration I have for my husband, Pride. You not only loved me through the hardest of days, but you helped me find the heartbeat of God so I could extend it to others. Your life is love in action.

I am appreciative of all who shared your stories with me, and to Marge, Arline, and Alice for sharing your lives with me.

Most of all, I would like to thank Evelyn, Stanley, and Rita Rossi for the privilege of walking with you on your journey Home. This is your story.

CONTENTS

Introduction 11

PART ONE: WHO SHALL GO?
1. Send Me 17
2. Hope 25
3. The Preparation 33
4. Unlikely Converts 43

PART TWO: WHAT YOU NEED ALONG THE WAY
5. A Road Map *(Know the Destination)* 55
6. Sturdy Shoes *(For the Rugged Terrain)* 64
7. GPS *(To Keep You on Track)* 69
8. Emergency Information
   (The Documents You Will Need) 72
9. Traveler's Assistance *(When You Feel Lost and Weary)*. . .79

PART THREE: NO TURNING BACK
10. Spiritual Warfare 99
11. Endurance 107
12. God's Covenant Love 115
13. Making Arrangements 126

PART FOUR: JOURNEY'S END
14. The Invisible Work 135
15. Giving Gifts 138
16. Physical Changes 143
17. The Home Going 156
18. Grieving Well 162

Appendix 170

"We will have all of eternity to celebrate the victories, but only a few hours before sunset to win them."

—AMY CARMICHAEL

INTRODUCTION

Today is one of those clear, crisp autumn days that reminds me that summer has said its final farewell for the year. A twinge of sadness accompanies this changing of the seasons not only because I hate to relinquish the long dog days of warmth and sunshine but also because this is the time of year when my mother died. All the trappings of fall, from the slight bite in the air to the changing colors of foliage, are hopelessly and irrevocably intertwined with the events surrounding the last days of her life.

On a strikingly beautiful morning so similar to this one, we sat at her kitchen table for what would be our last cup of coffee together, remarking about the beauty of the burnished maple tree across the street. So many hospital trips—including the last, after which she came home to die—were on days like today, when the leaves had just begun falling. Her final breath was taken on a day like this, when the sun, though low in the brilliant sapphire sky, was warm enough to make us thankful it wasn't yet winter.

Because there are a thousand memories such as these hanging in the gallery of my mind, all with the backdrop of a beautiful autumn day, the sights, smells, and the slight chill in the air at this time of year take me back to all that happened during that season of my mother's passage Home. I feel again the weight I shouldered. The constant physical, emotional, and spiritual challenges of caring for someone who was dying took an enormous toll on me, as did living with the continual throbbing heartache of knowing I would soon be losing someone I loved very much. Those experiences are now gone, but their pain was so real it is still almost tangible.

Though it is impossible to reflect upon these experiences without acknowledging the difficulties, sorrow, and fear that accompanied them, other memories of that last autumn of my mother's life have a completely different feeling. These are the memories most dear to me and that have given me the perspective of hope—and even gratitude—surrounding the profound experience we call death.

As I prepared to deal with the deepest of all human losses, there emerged a gift so sacred that it made the struggle bearable, even worthwhile. At the same time my mother's body was beginning to shut down before my eyes, her spirit, which had previously been diseased with bitterness and anger, began to find its way to life and health. The disappointments and injuries that had caused her to shut her heart to God seemed to ebb away from the shore of her soul. As she faced the end of her physical life, she finally found the impetus to reach out to the Lord—in a way I had never dreamed possible. What couldn't take place in the routine of living finally came about in the process of dying. As we shared that last autumn together, I had the distinct impression that I was not witnessing a death but rather a birth.

Almost one year to the day after my mother died from bladder cancer, Rita, my stepmother of nearly thirty years, took her last breath. Sixteen months after that, my father died. Within only twenty-eight months, all three of them were gone. None had been Christians before becoming ill, but all three came to Christ before dying. Tragically, some people will die without coming to faith. However, in the case of my parents, none of whom were likely candidates for giving their hearts to Christ, God used the dying process itself to bring about their conversions. As they struggled with the indignities of a deteriorating body, they were finally able to understand they were created to be eternal. Their deathbed became the cathedral in which they finally found peace with the Lord.

When an unbeliever is nearing death, we Christians understand better than anyone else that the stakes are high. We may not know exactly what to do, but we know something must be done. If we have not been accustomed to sharing our faith, doing so now may be uncomfortable. And if the person is quite close to us, or has been hostile toward God, we may be completely at a loss to know how to talk about our faith, even though we want the person to be able to understand how important faith is. We may be tempted to leave a copy of *The Four Spiritual Laws* by the bedside when no one is looking, or call in the pastor, hoping he can "close the deal." Though God sometimes uses these methods, more often He chooses everyday circumstances played out by people who have some kind of relationship with the dying person and who are willing to reflect Christ's love, even in the smallest ways.

When my parents were dying, I learned the power of serving. Listening to the words of my Christian mentors, I learned to "find a need and fill it." Initially, this took the form of going to doctor's appointments, running errands, and making meals. Later, as illness intensified, I had opportunities to serve in more challenging ways. Over time God used these acts to disarm the lifetime of arguments my parents had built against Him. Every time I showed up and quietly attended to something that needed to be done, I gained credibility in otherwise skeptical eyes and was granted access to souls that might have been shut to me and to my message of a Savior. Because Jesus came to the world as a servant, it makes total sense that He would use this technique as a powerful way to reach the lost.

The purpose of this book is to help you become an instrument through which God can minister to the spiritual needs of a dying person who does not yet know Him. You may be called to do nothing more than pray, and prayer is indeed a crucial component. Or you may be more involved, even to the point of becoming the primary caregiver. Whatever your role, I urge you to find a need and fill it. Someone whom you love is on the most difficult journey that can ever be taken. This person is lost, but you know the Way. For a little while you have the opportunity to walk along together. God may even use you to intercept the course, to change the destination, and to walk the person all the way Home to Him.

PART ONE

Who Shall Go?

CHAPTER 1

Send Me

*Then I heard the voice of the Lord, saying, "Whom shall
I send, and who will go for Us?" Then I said,
"Here am I. Send me!"*
—Isaiah 6:8

It all began with Marge. This was, in fact, the most unlikely of all beginnings, for although Marge and I had known each other for many years, we were acquaintances, really, and not what one would call close friends. Therefore, I never would have anticipated having such an intimate and powerful visit with her before she died. It was a moment that would change us both forever, and that would later have a huge impact on people whom we both loved very much.

Marge and her husband, George, were best friends and business partners of my father and stepmother, Rita. Unlike many people who work together, these four friends were inseparable. In 1972, when Dad and Rita were married in a Las Vegas wedding chapel, George and Marge were there with them, and more than thirty years later, they were still fast friends. They socialized together, vacationed together, celebrated most holidays together, and seemed to never tire of one another's company.

Marge was like a perfect *crème brûlée*. Inside she was sweet, soft, and somewhat delicate, but on the outside she was a bit crusty. Though she could swear like a sailor, it was never to inflict hurt but only for emphasis or to add color to a story. Her sense of humor was probably her predominant trait, and she saw the opportunity for laughter in almost every situation. Even the most mundane occurrence became hysterically funny when she would relay it to others. She was often the cause of side-splitting laughter for anyone within earshot of her tales, though no one could laugh more robustly than she.

Marge also loved practical jokes. I worked for her my first summer out of high school. At the end of August, when I was getting ready to leave for college, she masterminded a going-away party for me. A sumptuous, homemade chocolate sheet cake was the centerpiece of our little gathering, and I was coaxed into cutting the cake while everyone around smiled supportively.

With the knife in hand, I pantomimed how I would divide up the baked rectangle to ensure the proper number of pieces. After these calculations, I carefully plunged the knife. Much to my surprise, the cake resisted, and the knife sprung back! I took another pass, with even greater pressure, but still couldn't complete the incision. Thinking there must be a dreadful cook in our midst, I tried everything I could think of to cut this ill-formed confection without incriminating the poor baker, who would surely be humiliated.

When I began to hear snickers, I looked up at my co-workers and realized the entire scene was a ruse. As I cut, poked, sawed, and even stabbed, the cake simply would not give way. This was because my "cake" was really a piece of upholstery foam that had been cleverly decoyed with a luscious layer of chocolate frosting! Though no one ever took credit for putting that cake together, Marge's reputation for practical jokes made her the prime suspect, and everyone knew she was guilty as charged.

Through the years, I continued to see Marge at family gatherings, or whenever I would drop into the office to visit Dad and Rita. I admired Marge on many levels. She was a fine business-woman, wife, mother, grandmother, and a good friend to my father and stepmother. But it was how she dealt with pain that impressed me most.

Marge suffered from debilitating rheumatoid arthritis. As she aged, her condition worsened. Her hands and feet became severely gnarled and twisted, and just one look at her mangled joints gave a clear picture of the suffering she endured on a daily basis. Marge was one of those people who took everything—including pain—in stride. She *never* complained. Nor did she become irritable or take her hardship out on anyone else. She chose laughter instead. Marge was amazingly courageous, and because of her bravery, I had tremendous respect for her.

There came a time, though, when courage and laughter were not enough to sustain Marge. Her body and immune system were breaking down, and she caught one infection after another. When she was hospitalized for pneumonia three times within just a few months, we all knew it was the beginning of a serious downward trend.

Dad and Rita kept me informed of Marge's condition, but I lived too far away to be involved. Besides, she was *their* friend. I was, of course, sad to hear about her failing health, but it didn't really affect *me*.

At that time, I was teaching middle school in Los Angeles. During school one day, I suddenly had a very strong sense I *had* to go visit Marge, who was in the hospital. I knew I needed to see her face to face, spend time with her, and then pray with her. Since I had never prayed with Marge in my life, and didn't know whether this would be greeted warmly, I tried everything I could to shake that feeling. However, the urge was so strong and com-pelling, I couldn't deny it. I suspected (and hoped) this was the Holy Spirit leading, and though I wasn't totally sure, I didn't want to risk missing an appointment He had set. So on a Monday afternoon, immediately after school, I set out in the worst of rush hour traffic to visit Marge in a hospital in Orange County, nearly two hours away.

While driving, I began to have serious doubts about what I was doing. First of all, Marge and I had never talked about God—*ever*. I knew nothing of her religious background, and didn't even know if she believed in prayer. Who was I to come barging into her hospital room and announce it was time to pray? Besides, I was younger than her children and she probably wouldn't even take me seriously. Even if she were willing, I was sure George, Dad, and Rita would all be there, doing their best to distract Marge and keep the atmosphere lighthearted. It would be virtually impossible for me to walk in, take charge, and hold a prayer meeting. What was I thinking? Still I felt compelled to go, so I set out on my mission.

Lord, please let Marge be alone when I get there, I prayed while I was driving. As I envisioned the scene, my heart began to pound loudly. I really wanted to pray with and for Marge, and yet I just didn't know if I would be able to do it. It would be hard enough to do if we were alone, but if anyone else—especially my father or stepmother—were in the room with us, I would be petrified! *Lord, please!*

Something else worried me. I knew Marge had been hooked up to a breathing tube. If it were still in place, she wouldn't be able to speak. This would turn our visit into a monologue, perhaps leaving Marge with a feeling that she had been "ambushed." I envisioned myself stammering to her about God, and making a complete fool of myself. *God, if this is from you, I need your help!* Holding my doubts at bay, I decided to just go through with it and worry about the consequences later.

When I got out of my car in the hospital parking lot, I felt weak in the knees. How was I going to do this? I entered the hospital lobby, checked with the receptionist to find out Marge's room number, and stepped into the elevator. The ride seemed eternal.

As I headed toward Marge's room, memories of my own experience as a patient came flooding back to me. Five years ear-

lier, I had nearly died due to complications of what was sup-
posed to be a "minor" surgery and then spent nearly a year bed-
ridden. I knew full well the misery of living in a body that was
not functioning properly. With a twinge of sadness, I thought
about how lonely and isolated I had felt in the hospital, and how
grateful I was for every person who made time to come see me.
Visitors broke the monotony of what seemed interminable days
away from home. Whatever happened, perhaps Marge would at
least be glad to have some company.

I sighed with relief as I entered the room, for Marge was in
fact alone. She was awake, and her eyes lit up with the old twinkle as she recognized me. My hunch had been right! She was
clearly glad to have a visitor. She reached out for my hand and I
leaned over the bed in order to give her a full embrace. It *was*
good to see her.

I searched for a way to begin. "Marge, I was expecting to see
a breathing tube." In a raspy whisper, she explained that just
moments before I arrived, the doctor had asked George, Dad,
and Rita to leave so he could remove the tube. So far God had
taken care of every detail. *Thank you, Lord, for removing the tube
and for using that to clear the room. Your timing is perfect!*

Anyone who has been intubated experiences temporary irri-
tation of the vocal cords after the tube is removed, and speaking
becomes laborious. Marge's voice was barely audible, and in
order to hear her, I sat on her bed right beside her, holding her
frail hand in mine. I had to read her lips or put my ear almost
against her mouth in order to understand her hushed words.
Then I would pull back so she could see my face as I responded.
We "chatted" in this manner as well as we could. Ironically, the
obstacles served to create an intimacy we might not otherwise
have experienced. We spoke of her condition, and then of lighter
things that offered much needed comic relief. As usual, Marge
was keeping a stiff upper lip and tried to be as positive as
possible.

All through the visit, I prayed under my breath and looked
for my opportunity to divulge the reason I had really come. My

hope that Marge would be eager for human contact had proven to be true; perhaps I would be blessed again. Knowing Marge's circle of friends, I suspected I might be the only one who had come to offer prayer. I hoped she would welcome this change of pace.

Finally there was a lull in our pleasantries and I knew it was time. I squeezed her hand, looked straight into her eyes, and said, "Marge, I have come to do something that no one else in your life can do for you. Do you know what that is?" I think I startled her, and her brown eyes grew big with curiosity. "Marge, I want to pray for you. Would you like that?"

Suddenly, her eyes moistened, and I sensed a deep spiritual thirst in her. My heart leaped inside me, and I realized it had most assuredly been the Holy Spirit leading me to come here. Emboldened by Marge's openness, I leaned very close to her ear and prayed words that seemed to come from outside of me.

It was a prayer for her soul more than for her body. I asked God to be real to her, to be present with her, and to answer all the questions that were on her heart. I prayed for peace, for comfort, and for eternal hope. I prayed a long prayer, wondering all the while if perhaps it was too long. Knowing she was receiving numerous medications, I suspected she might fall asleep, but I kept on praying anyway. I prayed everything that was on my heart, and while I prayed, the sweetness of the Holy Spirit began to permeate the room.

When I finished, Marge was crying, holding tightly to me. After she regained her composure, she seemed to be searching for words. Her eyes were filled with wonder and awe when she said, "He's been here. I've seen *Him*." As she spoke, her tears flowed anew. "I didn't want to tell anyone."

My mind could scarcely take this in. I had hesitated to come, thinking my visit would be an intrusion or perhaps an opportunity for my own embarrassment. Yet long before I had the idea to come see Marge, God had been at work, revealing himself to her in this very room!

"Marge, if you saw Him, He is trying to tell you something.

He must have sent me here today to help you. You can have His peace right now. Do you want to know how to receive it?" She nodded.

I had been terrified of this visit and hadn't known what I would say. I simply knew I *must* come. Now here I was, sitting on the bed of a dying woman, talking with her about Jesus as though we had done this every day for years. It suddenly seemed easy and natural. By the time I left, I was certain the Holy Spirit had arranged the entire evening. I nearly floated out of the hospital to the parking lot.

As I drove home in the silent darkness of the freeway, I knew God had sent His radiant light into the heart of one woman in a hospital room. My earlier sense of icy dread had melted, giving way to the beautiful warmth of purpose and oneness with Christ. I knew I had witnessed a miracle, and that angels were rejoicing over what had taken place. Our conversation had far exceeded anything I could have hoped for or even imagined, and I was overcome with joy for having been part of what God did in her life. He could have sent anyone, but He sent *me*.

Marge died a few weeks later. At her funeral, George thanked me profusely for coming to see her in the hospital, and told me how much our time of prayer had meant to her. His expression of gratitude was deeply moving as was the fact that Marge had obviously relayed the whole story to him. It had no doubt been a very significant event for her. But even as George spoke and conveyed to me the most sincere appreciation, I knew it was not Marge but I who had received the most during our time together. God had used her to touch me in a profound and life-changing way, and to begin a work in me that would eventually spill out onto the lives of others. Some of them would be Marge's dearest friends.

Marge taught me that people come to the end of life spiritually thirsty. The dying process, though painful on so many levels, brings a new understanding that the physical world is not the complete picture and allows the person time to contemplate the significance of this. Though some may fight against God until the very end, there are many who, like Marge, are ready to drink at the Well. For them, illness and death are not an end but a beginning. As we offer a cup of cold water to them in the name of Jesus, the Lord can use it to quench even the deepest thirst.

CHAPTER 2

Hope

The Lord is not slow about His promise, as some count slowness, but is patient toward you, not wishing for any to perish but for all to come to repentance.
—2 PETER 3:9

Because you are reading this book, it is safe to assume that someone you know is dying. If so, you have some really important questions that need to be answered—*now*! I understand time is extremely limited—both for the person who is ill, and also for you if you are at all involved in caring for that person. My goal is to give you all the information you need and to do it in a way that honors those important time constraints.

If we could meet in person, as I have had the chance to do with many friends and acquaintances who are facing the death of a loved one, we would chat for a while about all that is happening with the person for whom you are concerned. (In this book, I will often refer to that person as your *loved one*, a term often reserved for family members, even though that person might be a neighbor, friend, co-worker, or even, up until now, a stranger.) You might describe what is happening medically, tell me about your relationship and history with this person, as well as share your immediate concerns with me. I would let you know that I have been down this road several times, and would try to comfort you with some of the things I have learned along the way. If all went well, we would have that kind of instant rapport that is formed when two people share common experiences. If so, before we parted company, you would eventually come around to the two issues pressing most heavily on your heart: (1) You know this person is not spiritually ready to die, and (2) you don't know what to do about it.

In our face-to-face chat, we could talk about a thousand other things, but these are the two that would be of utmost concern to you, and rightfully so. The medical issues, legal issues, and challenges of strained relationships will all eventually fade away, but the spiritual issues around death are the ones that matter most. So then, in that imaginary personal visit of ours, if you found you trusted me, these issues are the ones we would spend time discussing. I would try to impress on you the great significance of what you are doing and would pray for you. Then I would probably give you every possible way to contact me and let you know I would be available to coach you, pray for you, or encourage you in any way I could.

Books are different from conversations. Here we can't luxuriate in a two-way verbal interchange. I don't have any background on your personal situation or that of your loved one. Face to face, you would probably at least feel inclined to sit and listen awhile out of politeness, but you can put this book down at any time if I am not able to give you what you need. That's why I am going to dispense with anything superfluous that will waste your time, and get to the really important issues right away.

I know firsthand that the deathbed is the most fertile of all mission fields. Later on I will share the stories of people close to me who came to the Lord while they were dying (including my parents). I will also relate what others have told me about loved ones who have come to Christ during the last days of their lives.

But for now, I want to address the most pressing issues and thereby offer the hope you need to keep going *today*.

I know this person is not spiritually ready to die. For the most part, when someone is spiritually prepared for death, it shows in a sense of calm and peace. If these are not present, there is still some work to be done. However, there is no need for panic, which is for the most part very unproductive. The person may not be ready *now*, but that doesn't mean he or she can't be ready right on time! If you have ever been in a car accident or experienced any other serious trauma, you may know that feeling of time slowing down. Every second is elongated, and just a few moments seem to last forever. As a person prepares to die, something similar happens. Even if the person is very near death, God is still in control and hard at work on behalf of your loved one.

> Be anxious for nothing, but in everything by prayer and supplication with thanksgiving let your requests be made known to God.
> —PHILIPPIANS 4:6

It is easy to confuse being "right with the Lord" with outward signs, such as being baptized, attending church, tithing, and living a moral life. All of these are evident in the lives of mature believers; however, babes in Christ may not demonstrate these immediately. Therefore, as you share Christ's love with a dying person, it may be helpful to remember the thief on the cross. His conversion occurred immediately before death, and there was no time for the growth that would allow those outward evidences of his faith. Still, Jesus provided clear assurance that the thief would join his Master in paradise that very day. Missionaries say it takes years, sometimes a generation, for brand-new converts to reach maturity. Since there won't be that much time for this person, it is all right to focus on the bare essentials.

I don't know what to do.

It is completely natural not to know what to do when anyone is dying, especially if the person is an unbeliever. You may be uncomfortable around sickness and death, or you may feel paralyzed by the thought of losing someone you love. Perhaps you have never openly shared your faith with anyone before and don't know where to begin. Or perhaps you have led thousands to Christ but are suddenly aware of how difficult it can be to share faith with someone you have known for a long time. There are a hundred reasons why you might feel awkward, helpless, unqualified, or unfit to carry out the task at hand. Well, there's good news for you! The Bible is filled with ordinary people who felt exactly the same way, and God used all of them to do *amazing* things. Coming to the realization that you are inadequate for the job is not negative but very positive, for it will make it much easier for you to rely completely on the Lord.

In the months, days, or hours left before your loved one dies, you will discover it is not *your* responsibility to save that soul. That is the job of the Holy Spirit, and anything done apart from Him will fail. He is the One who knows what to do, and ideally, you are simply going to become a conduit through which He can act. So if you feel you don't know what to do, rejoice! This means you are ready to completely surrender to whatever God has in mind.

> Abide in Me, and I in you. As the branch cannot bear fruit
> of itself, unless it abides in the vine, so neither can you,
> unless you abide in Me.
> —JOHN 15:4

> But the Helper, the Holy Spirit, whom the Father will
> send in My name, He will teach you all things, and bring
> to your remembrance all that I said to you.
> —JOHN 14:26

Let's look at a few other questions you might be contemplating. Each one of these will be dealt with in greater detail later on, but I would like to give cursory attention to them here. The most common questions fall into the standard categories of Who? What? Why? When? Where? How?

Who?

This question can sometimes be translated *"Not me, Lord!"* Joseph, Moses, Joshua, Gideon, Hannah, David, Daniel, the prophets, Mary, Peter, Paul, and even the boy with two fish and five loaves could have said this very thing! They didn't feel prepared for what was coming and knew there would be great costs involved. They might have thought they didn't have the credentials, experience, or courage for the task at hand, but God called each of them to perform that task. This is true for you, too, and He will give you *everything* you need to accomplish His purpose. As someone has put it, *He doesn't call the equipped, but equips the called.*

> I searched for a man among them who should build up the wall and stand in the gap before Me for the land, so that I should not destroy it; but I found no one.
> —EZEKIEL 22:30

> Not that we are adequate in ourselves to consider anything as coming from ourselves, but our adequacy is from God.
> —2 CORINTHIANS 3:5

What?

What is going to happen? What can I expect? What chance is there for this person to come to the Lord? In chapter 16, I will explain exactly what can be expected as death comes closer. Having some knowledge about the signs of death and about the timeline will take away some of the mystery and fear and will help you gauge the time. Between now and then, there is much to be done, and the possibilities are incredible! Yes, there is a lot at stake, but there has never been a better opportunity for your loved one to come to faith! Illness has a way of making a person hungry for the truth about spiritual matters. At the same time,

Jesus Christ himself is interceding for this person. He wants to see a change even more than you do. Leave the outcome in His hands and be obedient to the part He wants you to play.

He is able, once and forever, to save those who come to God through him. He lives forever to intercede with God on their behalf.
—HEBREWS 7:25 NLT

"I will have mercy on whom I have mercy, and I will have compassion on whom I have compassion." So then it does not depend on the man who wills or the man who runs, but on God who has mercy.
—ROMANS 9:15–16

Why?

Why is this happening? It is heartbreaking to watch someone we love suffer with illness. Sometimes it raises difficult questions for us and can even make us feel angry with, or abandoned by, God. Though we can't always know why He chooses a certain path for us, we can trust Him based on what we know of His character. If the situation seems unbearable, reflect on what these hardships are purchasing in eternity. No matter how deep the suffering, the cost is nothing compared to the joy that will be experienced if your loved one comes to know Jesus through this ordeal.

So we fix our eyes not on what is seen, but on what is unseen. For what is seen is temporary, but what is unseen is eternal.
—2 CORINTHIANS 4:18 NIV

When?

When will God do something? Will there be enough time? How long will it take? The great paradox of terminal illness is that while we are waiting for something to happen, time seems to be both too long and too short. The dying process can move at the speed of a glacier. Though the changes are sometimes imperceptible, they carve out deep gorges in our lives and require every last ounce of endurance that can be mustered. We may become impatient, exhausted, or frustrated, longing for something to happen. And yet arriving at the finish line means that someone we love is taken from us, an outcome we dread and want postponed as long as possible. While we are caught between wanting something to happen and fearing that it might, we need to remember that time, whether it is moving rapidly or in slow motion, is in God's hands. The minutes are irrelevant to Him, and He is capable of making everything take place perfectly, at the moment He has appointed. When you are able to look back on the situation, this will come into perfect focus.

Let us not lose heart in doing good, for in due time we shall reap if we do not grow weary.
—GALATIANS 6:9

He has made everything beautiful in its time. Also He has put eternity in their hearts.
—ECCLESIASTES 3:11 NKJV

Where?

Where will God work? When life, death, and eternity are on the line, God's methods of working seem to take on a new fluidity. You won't have to wait for the "right setting" in order to speak to your loved one, but may find that the most perfect time comes in unlikely, or even unorthodox, surroundings. You may be able to pray with someone in an elevator, or speak about God's love while you are in a doctor's office. You may be at home, in the hospital, or even the grocery store when the Holy Spirit moves. Keep your mind open, and remember that most of what is going to take place will be within the heart of the other person and will be completely invisible to you. God can use any setting to fulfill His purpose, so be on the alert and be sensitive to a softening spirit.

At whatever place you hear the sound of the trumpet,
rally to us there. Our God will fight for us.
—NEHEMIAH 4:20

The eyes of the Lord are in every place.
—PROVERBS 15:3

How?

How will God use me? Recently I took a trip to the Philippines to visit missionaries working with Wycliffe Bible Translators. I was amazed to see how many different types of missionaries there are! Administrators, accountants, bookkeepers, office personnel, schoolteachers, librarians, computer experts, construction workers, medical staff, and of course, linguists are all needed for the work of Bible translation. In the mission community, every role is seen as essential, and those who are performing the actual Bible translation are not elevated above those who are serving in supportive roles. There is an understanding that one cannot exist without the other.

The work of sharing Christ's love with the dying is similar. While the main objective is to introduce the person to Christ, the small, seemingly unimportant duties are often what allow this to be accomplished. Instead of talking directly about God, you may first find yourself providing a meal or transportation. Ordinary tasks such as these have incredible impact on an unbeliever, and often, sharing the Gospel cannot otherwise happen.

God will reveal to you how He wants to use you to share His love. For now, the most important thing you can do is decide to walk along with the person for a little while. So put on your shoes and trust that everything will be made clear to you as you travel.

Do you not know that those who run in a race all run, but
only one receives the prize? Run in such a way that you
may win.
—1 CORINTHIANS 9:2

And looking upon them Jesus said to them, "With people
this is impossible, but with God all things are possible."
—MATTHEW 19:26

CHAPTER 3

The Preparation

*For we are God's masterpiece. He has created us anew
in Christ Jesus, so we can do the good things
he planned for us long ago.*
—EPHESIANS 2:10 NLT

My mom was as tough as they come. Barely over five feet tall, she was a little fireball, as strong as steel inside and out. Though she eventually became quite the intellectual, she grew up on a small backwoods Arkansas farm and took great pride in being able to do *anything*. She would never think of hiring someone to perform household repairs, and well into her seventies she could still get up on her own roof to replace shingles. She had figured out early in life that the only person she could totally rely on was herself, and she didn't need *anyone* else—including God.

How can the Holy Spirit work on a heart that is barricaded within such a strong fortress of self-sufficiency? Often He uses illness. There is no amount of competency, no mental or physical prowess that can ward off the terrifying reality of a health crisis. Most of us think we are impervious to disaster, and when we come face to face with our own mortality, we suddenly understand how truly frail we are. Not even my mother was immune to this.

She had known something was wrong and had ignored it. For months she had experienced frightening changes in her body and was hoping to will them away. When she finally told me what was happening, I was aghast she hadn't sought medical advice much sooner. Once we finally began the arduous task of finding out what was wrong, we almost didn't want to know.

It was strange to see my mother, the spitfire, immobilized and afraid. I had watched her go through a bitter divorce and seen her struggle to raise my brother and me by herself. She had worked to build her prestigious career as a university professor and had breezed over enormous hurdles that would have derailed many women of her era. Once she had even witnessed a brutal murder in her workplace and had been the only person with the presence of mind to take action. Nothing ever shook her—until now. The woman who had always amazed me with her cool, calm strength was unraveling before my eyes. She was suddenly looking to me, hoping I could fix everything.

The truth is, I was scared, too. I had no idea what lay ahead, and I had never contemplated life without my mother there. I didn't want to lose her, but I became aware that I might have to face that possibility. While I waited for her diagnosis, life took on a thick, slow-motion heaviness. When the diagnosis came, everything else screeched to a halt. Once I could breathe again, I looked around me and realized I was in totally foreign territory.

HOW GOD PREPARES US

My life dramatically changed the day my mother was diagnosed with cancer. I think it is like that for everyone, whether the news is cancer, heart attack, stroke, an accident, or any other life-threatening condition. We might try to appear unaffected and attempt to go along with business as usual, but inside we know this is a watershed moment. Life is going to be defined in two segments: what came before the diagnosis, and what came after.

For me, it began in a hospital waiting room. It seemed to happen too suddenly, not giving me enough time to prepare. As I contemplated the weight of the situation, I sensed this was the start of a completely different life. But that was not where it all really began.

Long before I was born, or even before my mother was born, God knew what was going to take place in that hospital waiting room. He was never left breathless, never stunned, never caught off guard. He was thoroughly prepared for it all, and in fact had planned it. He had every detail already in place before the beginning of time. For me, everything was spinning too quickly, but I didn't realize it wasn't spinning out of control. It was more like being at the hub of a wheel, where all the spokes of my life converged. This was exactly what God had intended.

GOD'S WAYS ARE HIGHER

Over my life, I have learned that God always has a purpose in things that seem bad at first glance. The word *cancer* seemed *really* bad! My mother had inoperable, stage-four cancer, which is the worst possible scenario. It would do no good to ask why God had allowed this or to let myself feel abandoned by Him. I couldn't afford the luxury of panic or self-pity. I needed to stay spiritually alert. In order to understand how to respond to these circumstances, I had to find the answer to one important question: *"What is God trying to accomplish?"*

Ironically, I would have to ask that same question in similar circumstances several more times in very short order. My mom was diagnosed with cancer in December 2000. A few months later my father had a serious stroke and was hospitalized for several months. He was released just weeks before cancer was found in his wife's liver. Meanwhile, a dear friend began losing her struggle with ovarian cancer. At one juncture, all four of them were in the hospital at the same time.

For a period of two and a half years, my life was utterly consumed with the illnesses and deaths of people I loved. Sometimes the load of sadness I carried was almost too much to bear. Throughout that extremely difficult season, I knew God had to be up to something. I had to try to be in sync with Him and see the situation as He saw it. If I could find out what He was trying to do, maybe I could survive. Instead of fighting the current, I needed to ride the wave.

Though part of me felt like a scared little girl, my parents increasingly began looking to me for answers and assistance. I sensed it was my turn to take the lead. I wanted to help them, but I wasn't sure how and didn't feel qualified to do anything that would make an impact. Still I kept wondering, *What is God trying to accomplish? Can He use me?*

The truth was, I *did* have something to give them. Although I didn't have medical training and wasn't a counselor or social worker, I knew the answers to the questions that really mattered. My faith automatically qualified me to deliver the goods they needed. I personally knew the only One who was going to be able to get them through their ordeal, and I could help them meet Him. My role was no longer the role of a daughter but that was what opened the door for me to participate. As I walked through that door, God would use me to help them in ways I couldn't yet imagine.

As I strained to see these circumstances with His eyes, His sovereignty began to come into focus. I had prayed for years for my parents to come to Christ. At one time I had almost given up, but had recently felt more of a burden on my heart for them. Maybe these life-and-death struggles were not tragedies at all but rather the answer to those prayers. If that were the case, I needed to discover how I could participate in what God was doing. I certainly didn't want to miss it!

FINDING THE PATH

Once I understood that God could use illness as a way to draw my parents to Him, I still needed to know specifically how

He could use me in the process. This meant I had to be honest with myself about how far I was willing to go on this journey and what roles I would be willing to fill. I also needed to look at my personality, my abilities, and my past experiences, to see if they offered clues as to what I had to offer my parents. Because there is no one-size-fits-all technique for sharing Christ's love with a dying person, these things helped me see ways I was already equipped for this work.

When God asks us to do something, He prepares us to be *able* to do it (that doesn't necessarily mean we will *feel* prepared!). One way God prepared me was through my own illness, six years before my mother's cancer diagnosis. I experienced what could best be referred to as a "surgical accident," one of those freaky, one-in-a-million slipups that the doctor says is highly unlikely. I nearly died, had an extended hospital stay, and then spent almost a year in bed. Though that ordeal was one of the most terrible events of my life, it helped me understand the frustrations and challenges of a health crisis. This knowledge became my starting place on the path that would eventually lead to my parents' salvation.

For example, when I was in the hospital, every inch of my body ached. Due to the huge anchor-shaped incision on my abdomen, I was forced to lie on my back in the same position, day after day. My shoulder and back muscles responded to this confinement with constant spasms, adding to the overall misery I was experiencing because of my deteriorating health. To make matters even worse, it was Christmas! I had never felt so low.

On Christmas Eve, my nurse quietly entered my room and asked if I would like to have my shoulders and back rubbed. I was surprised she had asked this, and wondered if she knew how much pain I had. Though I never would have asked her to do this, I gladly accepted her offer. As my knotted muscles began to unwind, I almost burst into tears. This nurse seemed to be my very own Christmas angel. Her simple act of kindness meant more to me than anything else that happened to me in the hospital. Later I found out she was a Christian, and I was so grateful that she had taken time to reach out to me. Now, more than ten years later, the memory of her action still causes me great emotion.

To the ill, even the smallest gesture can have a huge impact. My angel nurse did something very simple, but I will never forget it. Her kindness and caring set her apart from every other nurse and doctor I encountered. As it happened, we were of the same faith. Had that been different, I think I would have been willing to listen to anything she had to say because what she did earned her a place of honor and respect in my eyes. She not only ministered to me but she also taught me that one of the most powerful ways to gain entrance into someone's heart is to serve them. This point became the central theme of how I dealt with my parents while they were dying. Clearly God used my own illness as a way to prepare me to share Christ's love with my parents.

Your background and experiences are different than mine, but God will show you the unique ways He has already prepared you to minister to the person on your heart. If you are willing to be involved, there are innumerable ways for that to happen. All you need to do is look for points of contact. These will most often be tangible deeds you can perform to show care and concern. Unless you know the person will be spiritually open, there is no need to focus on offering prayer or Bible reading, at least not in the beginning. The person probably won't be ready. Instead, concentrate on everyday needs to which you can attend. Find ways to be useful and to *serve* in the name of Jesus. Try to recognize any burdens the person is carrying and see whether you can share in the load for a little while. These are the important first steps. As you take them, you will begin to see the path God has chosen for you.

The following pages contain questions designed to help you see ways God might have prepared you to share Christ's love with a dying person. Some will be things you haven't thought of or have overlooked as unimportant. They represent only a small portion of the innumerable ways God can use you and may help you brainstorm about other ideas that fit your own circumstances. There is no magic score sheet or key at the end that will tell you what to do next. These questions are for your reflection and to provide seeds for your own thinking. I urge you to spend time in prayer with these questions before you. Allow the Holy Spirit to tell you how He can use you to help accomplish the work He has already begun. If you have other ideas, be sure to jot them down. Soon you will begin to see patterns emerging and will come to conclusions about ways you can reach out in Christ's love. Your contribution will make all the difference.

FINDING YOUR PATH TO SERVICE

About You

1. If God asks you to do something for this person, are you willing to do it?
2. Are there limits on what you would be willing to do? What are they?
3. What do you think God might be asking you to do?
4. Will doing the above require any lifestyle changes for you?
5. How will helping this person affect your family (spouse, children, etc.)? Is your family in agreement with what you want to do?
6. What would it be worth to you to see this person again in heaven?
7. What is your greatest area of giftedness? Do you already know what your spiritual gifts are? How might God be able to use you in this situation?
8. Do you have any special abilities or talents? How might God be able to use these to help the person?
9. Have you had any special experiences that you think may have prepared you to help this person in some way?
10. What made you decide to read this book? Do you feel called to walk this person to the end of the journey?
11. Do you think God has called you to be involved with this person now?

12. What interests do you have in common with this person?
13. What is your fondest memory of being with this person? What was the connection point between you?
14. What about this person makes you laugh or feel happy?
15. What about this person makes you feel sad?
16. Do you have any memories about this person that are painful? Do you need to forgive the person for something? Does he or she need to forgive you? *(If so, it is important that you try to clear this up as soon as possible. It will not only distract you from what you are doing, but may make you ineffective.)*
17. Are there one or two ways in which you are similar to the person?
18. What are one or two ways you are different from this person?
19. If this person dies, how will his or her death affect you? Will your life be very different from what it is now?
20. What is your understanding of salvation, of heaven, and of hell?
21. Have you ever led a person to Christ? If not, are you willing to do so? Do you know how to do this?
22. Do you think there is anything about you or anything you have done that reflects Christ to this person?

About Your Loved One

1. How much has this person told you about his or her medical condition and prognosis? Is it appropriate for you to know more?
2. Does the person currently have medical insurance? If not, how will medical bills be paid?
3. Does the person currently have a source of emotional support? Who is it?
4. What do you think the person is most concerned about medically right now?
5. What do you think are the other concerns of the person? *(Common items include taking care of a spouse, children, a pet, or a home; paying bills; transportation to medical treatments;*

job concerns; drafting a will; estranged relationships; being alone.)

6. Are there any of the above items you can help tackle? Would this person be comfortable accepting your help?
7. Does the person value solitude and privacy or prefer to be surrounded by people?
8. Does the person enjoy fun, distracting activities outside of the house or prefer to stay close to home?
9. Does the person enjoy reading, watching movies, or listening to music?
10. Does the person enjoy humor? If so, in what ways?
11. Does the person enjoy gardening, nature, or the outdoors? Are there any ways to honor this interest during this time?
12. Are there pets that must be cared for? If not, might the person enjoy being around someone else's animals? *(Some hospitals have therapy pets available.)*
13. Is this person typically fastidious about his or her appearance? Will hospital gowns or the inability to groom or apply makeup be frustrating? How can you help?
14. Does the person have special dietary needs or is he or she a picky eater? Are you aware of any food restrictions and preferences? Can you provide some favorite foods and beverages?
15. If the person is in the hospital, are there any items from home that might be of comfort *(pillow, pajamas, slippers, books, crossword puzzles, music, etc.)*?
16. Does the person enjoy cards, flowers, and gifts?
17. Would this person be more likely to sense your caring through encouraging words, the use of physical touch, or through the time you spend with him or her?
18. Which of the above can you provide? How?
19. Was this person ever a victim of abuse or neglect? By whom?
20. Has the person ever been betrayed by someone close? Who was it?
21. What do you know about the person's understanding of God? Is there anger or disappointment in this area?

22. Has this person ever accepted Jesus Christ as his or her personal Savior?

Thought for reflection: If past hurt or resentment has existed between you and your loved one, you may find it difficult to reach out in love to that person. Emotional debris of this nature can rob you of a great opportunity and make you want to avoid the person now. Or you may have a subconscious expectation that during this process, you will experience resolution to unfinished business. While this is possible, often the other person is not capable of meeting you in this way. If you decide to walk with your loved one on this journey, it is best to do so without expecting anything in return. You may need to reflect on the past with an objective person to help gain perspective or journal about your feelings. In any case, it is never a good idea to bring your unfinished business into this arena. Try to table your own needs until after the person is gone. In the meantime, by sharing the love of Christ and following His example of service, you may find the healing you have been seeking.

CHAPTER 4

Unlikely Converts

*There is nothing, not even the devil himself, that can
hinder the confessing sinner.*
—A. W. TOZER

When people hear that my mother, father, and stepmother all came to the Lord while they were dying, they usually assume my parents had already been living with one foot in the kingdom. Their struggles with illness probably tipped the scales just enough to bump them over into the glory side before it was too late. Nothing could be further from the truth! My parents were the most unlikely converts of all, and for very different reasons each one was completely hostile toward Christ and the Gospel message. Over the years I had tried every way I knew to share my faith with them, but they made it clear I was never even to bring up the name of Jesus. He was not a welcome topic of discussion.

Frankly, I am still amazed my parents were able to embrace faith in Christ before they died, because their hearts were some of the hardest and most worldly I have ever seen. Yet if the Lord was able to do a work in *their* lives, there is certainly hope for the person you are holding in your heart, no matter the spiritual condition of that person today!

In this chapter, I will share my parents' backgrounds. Each of the three (I include my stepmother as a parent) had a unique story, with the only common element being their rejection of God in life and their salvation prior to death. It isn't important that these are the stories of my parents, for many people have shared with me about their loved ones coming to Christ at the end of life. It doesn't matter how far away the person is from the Lord or how unlikely a conversion seems. The Lord's mercies are new every morning (even the last morning), and as long as there is breath, there is hope.

> I remember my affliction and my wandering, the bitterness and the gall. I well remember them, and my soul is downcast within me. Yet this I call to mind and therefore I have hope: Because of the Lord's great love we are not consumed, for his compassions never fail. They are new every morning; great is your faithfulness. . . .
>
> For men are not cast off by the Lord forever. Though he brings grief, he will show compassion, so great is his unfailing love. . . . Why should any living man complain when punished for his sins? Let us examine our ways and test them, and let us return to the Lord.
>
> —LAMENTATIONS 3:19–23, 31–32, 39–40 NIV

THE KING OF THE NIGHT LIFE

My father was in the bar and nightclub business, and to put it mildly, he wasn't like any of the other fathers in our neighborhood. That much I knew. Oh, he was a good provider for our family, and we enjoyed affluence others may not have had. Most families we knew drove older Chevys, Buicks, or Volkswagens, but we got a brand-new Cadillac every other year like clockwork. Back in the days when we were still using 8-track tapes and phonographs to hear our favorite tunes, and long before built-in DVD players, my brother and I were the proud viewers of one of the first car televisions. My dad loved to flaunt his money, and so he enjoyed having us ride around town with our big rabbit-ear antenna sticking out the rear window of the Caddy.

My dad's chief goal in life was to be rich. He had grown up in the Great Depression and his family, like most during that time, had suffered greatly. He talked about being hungry and not being able to do anything about it. He was a star player on the high school football team, but few knew he had joined just to get the free shoes and sweat pants that came with being on the team. He didn't want to ever be in that position again, so he developed his entrepreneurial gifts as his ticket out of poverty. Before he graduated from Santa Barbara High, Dad had leveraged a deal whereby he and his brother would only play on the championship team if they could own half interest in the concession stand that operated during home games. Thus began my father's business career.

Dad was definitely a hard worker. The problem was his unique code of ethics. My Italian immigrant grandfather had been a bootlegger during Prohibition days, so Dad was accustomed to being around alcohol and illegal activity working in tandem. Early in life, he learned there was good money to be made by selling liquor, no matter how it was obtained. It wasn't too surprising that as a young man during World War II, my father was mysteriously able to procure enough whiskey to keep several bars in business, in spite of strict rationing rules that were in place during those days. He obviously had the right connections and knew how to use them.

My father owned and operated forty-two different bars during his career. He was great with people and loved the action associated with the night life, so his bars were always hot spots that drew big crowds. Dad's specialty was purchasing clubs that were losing money. He had a knack for redecorating them, giving them a new theme, and turning them into money-makers, often doubling his investment practically overnight. He was known for having the "Midas touch" because everything he touched turned to gold.

One of the bars Dad owned when I was very young was called "The Den." He enlisted the help of my mother, who was a pretty good artist, in that redecorating project. The two of them were busy one afternoon in our garage, working on some murals to hang in the new "joint." I had been warned not to disturb them, but late in the afternoon I couldn't stand the suspense any longer. I wanted to see what they were doing, so I quietly ventured into the garage. I was shocked to see several large canvas murals on which Mom had painted eerie scenes of nude men and women, each with a tail, pitchfork, and set of horns. They were surrounded by flames and sported strange, ghoulish grins that haunted me. Apparently the theme for "The Den" was a den of *devils*! Though I was probably only six or seven years old at the time, I shuddered at the sight of those pictures and felt ashamed of my parents for creating them.

My dad was proud of his bars and bragged about them all the time. I was suddenly mortified, wondering who else knew about these terrible pictures of naked men and women—or rather demons. Did my teachers and classmates know? Our neighbors? How about the family who had been taking me to church? My Sunday school teacher? I envisioned all the "regular" people in the community gathering together to discuss the poor little girl whose father was "in cahoots" with the devil. Maybe the faithful were holding secret prayer meetings for us.

I carried the weight of that shame around with me for years. As I grew older and could understand more, other things surfaced that added to that burden. For instance, Dad eventually added topless cocktail waitresses to spice things up a bit. Worse yet, I suspected he had a girlfriend. I grew up in the days when "family values" really were the norm, but in my own family there seemed to be no limits to what could happen. The only thing my dad valued was the dollar bill.

THE INTELLECTUAL

I often wondered how my mom and dad ended up married to each other. Their backgrounds and philosophies were so different that they made an unlikely match. Dad was lawless, and for him the ends always justified the means. Mom, on the other hand, was an intellectual and humanitarian. She had strong convictions about almost everything, especially right and wrong and how others should be treated. She had lofty ideals, but she had deliberately left God behind.

Mom had grown up in a strong Christian home. My grandparents were country people from Arkansas farmlands near the Ozark Mountains. They weren't educated or sophisticated, but they did love the Lord. Their brand of Christianity was very strict, incorporating doctrines with a lot of rules and regulations. This was all they knew. At the age of fifteen, Mom was sent to their denomination's high school in Kansas, where she had to work to earn her education, room, and board. There she got a full dose of what seemed to her to be extremely harsh dogma along with her first glimpses of religious hypocrisy. These started to chip away at her foundation of faith.

Mom's intellect was always her most prominent feature, so it was no wonder she graduated as valedictorian of her class. Afterward she made her way to California, where she attended Pasadena College, the predecessor to Point Loma (a Christian college in Southern California). She once again worked her way through school, earning both her degree and a teaching credential. While in Pasadena, she also met and married her first husband. Later I found out this failed marriage and subsequent divorce played a significant role in extinguishing any last spark of belief in God Mom still had.

Even to her dying day, my mother *never* mentioned her first marriage. I learned of it in bits and pieces from my aunts, mostly after Mom died. I understood why she chose not to talk about it, because that marriage was completely incongruent with the person she presented herself to be, a self-proclaimed agnostic.

When I was six, my mother reluctantly gave me permission to accept a neighbor's invitation to Sunday school. This opened up a whole new world to me and gave me respite from the dark atmosphere at home. As my involvement increased, my mother became more distant. She continued to let me go to church, but it was clear I was not to talk about God. I was seven years old when I accepted Christ, and I knew I couldn't tell her. It seemed she was angry with me or didn't like me anymore now that God was an important part of my life. I wondered why she hated God so much. How could I have known that her first marriage, a terribly unhappy one, had been to a pastor?

Whatever happened during those years before she met my dad, it left her terribly scarred and spiritually disabled. Apparently she and her husband had pastored a church together in Wisconsin, and things went wrong both in the church and in the marriage. As the story goes, her husband was harsh, the denomination was harsh, and people in the church seemed false. When she could bear it no more, she made a swift and complete break. In one fell swoop she left the marriage, her family's values, and God. There would be no turning back.

Mom probably married my dad in an attempt to get as far away from her Christian roots as possible. Some have said she was simply drawn to his good looks because she was seeking out the best gene pool for the children she so desperately wanted. In either case, her decision cost her a great deal. She wasn't cut out for the wild night life my dad enjoyed, and she detested his business practices. He, in turn, couldn't understand her highly principled way of looking at things or why she wouldn't "loosen up!" Though they stayed married for years, they lived in two completely different worlds. To escape, she went back to school and earned her doctorate in education. By the time she completed it, her marriage had ended.

My mother never fully recovered from her emotional wounds. Her professional career as a university professor flourished, but the windows to her soul became more and more clouded by isolation, bitterness, and anger. It was as though she had pulled the shade down to block out God and bitter memories, seemingly forever.

THE MATERIAL GIRL

Rita, my stepmom, was truly one-of-a-kind. Over the thirty years she was married to my father we became very close friends and enjoyed many good times together. But our relationship wasn't always so comfortable. In the beginning she was a cocktail waitress in one of my dad's clubs, and their relationship blossomed long before my parents were divorced. She was hysterically funny, spontaneous, and loved excitement of every kind. These qualities, plus the fact that she was twenty years younger than my mother, made her a formidable opponent. For a while my father led a double life, spending time with both families, but eventually opted to join Rita and her two children, leaving us behind.

My loyalties, of course, remained with my mother. For years I would have nothing to do with my dad, and especially not with Rita, who was simply referred to as "her." I wasn't sure whether the bitterness was my own or my mother's (or maybe a little of both), but it took years to overcome. Had I known Rita under different circumstances, I probably would have liked her immediately.

Rita was a pleasant, warm, and very giving person. In fact, she would literally give you the shirt off her back—especially if that meant she could go shopping for a new one! She did a lot of thoughtful things for other people, and she had a good time wherever she went. But Rita lived for the here and now, not for any "pie in the sky." What mattered to her were things she could touch.

Rita grew up in Beverly Hills, and had a taste for the finer things in life. Though she attended parochial school and went to mass regularly with her family, she wasn't interested in religion or God. In fact, her biggest obstacle to having a personal faith was her religious upbringing. She hated cheap imitations, even in the church. She knew too many people who considered themselves "good Catholics" (meaning they attended mass and confession regularly) but whose everyday life practices revealed souls as small and shriveled as the Grinch's. She thought priests and nuns were old-fashioned, and for the most part she ignored their teachings. Still, she never begrudged anyone their beliefs, and felt people had the right to delude themselves with nice little fairy tales if they wanted to. That was fine for them. She, on the other hand, would keep her feet firmly on planet earth and grab everything she could while she was here.

I suppose I never fully expected my mother, father, or Rita to understand or embrace a personal faith in Jesus Christ. I had dreamed it would somehow happen, just as I hoped for happy endings to all the chapters in my life. But their conversions seemed highly unlikely, and on some level, I think I had given up.

As each of these three very different people faced illness and death, their responses were surprisingly similar. Initially, they fully expected the doctors to make them well again. They explored all the options and fought with great determination to live. When finally there were no more options, they became reconciled to the fact that they were losing the battle. It was only then that their clenched fists gave way to open hands—hands that were ready to take hold of the Savior. For them, the path to faith couldn't have happened any other way.

This pattern is common among those who are terminally ill. The struggle to survive is often followed by a time of relinquishment. But somewhere in between, the person comes face to face with his or her own mortality and realizes, perhaps for the very first time, that life in this world will come to an end. This is the intersection where even the most ardent skeptic begins to look for spiritual truth and may be willing to trade in a lifetime of doubt for newfound faith.

Don't be discouraged by how unlikely it seems for your loved one to come to Christ. There have been others, far less likely, who have turned completely around in their thinking. This journey into illness will have immeasurable impact on your loved one's soul, which is precisely why it is so important for you to be available to walk alongside him or her during this struggle. You already know the Truth, and when your loved one comes to that important crossroad, your words and guidance will help lead the way.

If you do not see evidence yet that your loved one is open to the Gospel, don't despair. Instead, be patient. Look for ways to minister to physical needs, and never insist upon talking about spiritual things. But all the while, keep your eyes and ears open to notice small changes that signal spiritual openness is on the horizon. These changes (we will talk about them more in the next chapter) are significant landmarks on your journey, and until you begin to see them, you can easily become discouraged. Instead, think about any long trip you have taken to some incredible destination. You wouldn't give up on seeing the Grand Canyon just because you had to cross miles and miles of desert first. You would trust others who had been there and follow their directions in order to see one of the most amazing places in the world. Eventually the terrain would change and you would know that what you were longing to see was getting nearer. This journey is the same. Keep going. It will be worth it!

PART TWO

What You Need
Along the Way

CHAPTER 5

A Road Map
(Know the Destination)

One road leads home and a thousand roads
lead into the wilderness.
—C. S. LEWIS

This journey is different from any other you will ever take. Though it will leave you changed, it is not *your* journey. Rather, you are walking alongside someone else who is discovering the ultimate destination. The person whose journey it is must set the course and take the lead. This is not yours to do. You are there to offer support and lighten the load when you can—not to steer. However, if the person is not a believer, you are keenly aware that the chosen route leads directly into the wilderness. For a time you must proceed knowing this, and simply love the traveler, offer good company, and prove your faithfulness. Your hope is that your loved one will eventually realize the road has led nowhere and will at last turn to you for direction. Only then will you be able to show the Way. It is important that you consult the map in advance so you will know exactly where to go when that time comes.

If you want to see the one you love reach Home safely, it won't work to force the traveler onto your route, even though you know where it leads. Your loved one will resent this. By pressing the issue, you may hinder the work of the Holy Spirit and prevent the very thing you want to happen.

WATCH FOR LANDMARKS

When my father was recovering from a massive stroke, he began, for the first time in our relationship, to reveal his inner heart to me. I believe this happened only because of the countless hours during which I sat with him at the hospital. Due to my teaching schedule at the University, my opportunities to see him often fell during parts of the day that were inconvenient for others. This provided us with great expanses of time to ourselves. He loved to tell stories, and I became his best audience, asking him to replay all the great accomplishments of his life and to delve into family history that I knew was soon to be lost. During those visits, he sized me up, and eventually decided I was safe. That was when he started asking questions about God. However, before he ever ventured into that territory, he managed to tell me that I used to be a "Bible thumper who preached sermons" to him. By doing so, he clearly informed me he was now interested in God, but wasn't going to respond to that approach.

Over time Dad became more transparent about spiritual matters and even opened up about his fears. His vulnerability was the first significant landmark on our journey, and signaled to me that we had passed into new territory. My father had been scrutinizing my every move, curious as to whether my concern for him had strings attached. Because I met him on his terms and showed up simply to love him, he was eventually satisfied I could be trusted. Both of us initially tiptoed over this boundary, but as we became more comfortable our conversations about God intensified. Later, when I offered to pray for him and read from the Bible, he was completely open. Eventually he made the requests for prayer and Bible readings, once again providing an important landmark in his spiritual journey. Though I was always mindful of the pace that was comfortable for him, I took note of the cues he gave me that indicated he was ready to go to a new level.

As you look for or encounter opportunities to speak to your loved one about the Lord, remember that old perspectives and viewpoints may now be in a state of change. You may assume you know the person's beliefs and boundaries, but because they are shifting, you may misjudge what you can or cannot say. You may also find that former objections, even though strongly held in the past, no longer matter and are replaced by a new openness.

If your loved one provides you with a spiritual landmark, it is important for you to respond in a way that will facilitate further discussion. Otherwise, the query (even if veiled) will just dangle in space, and the opportunity will be lost. This requires a great deal of respect, reverence, and restraint in order to avoid shutting down the conversation altogether. This is a time to listen more than you speak, to gather rather than dispense information.

Think of these landmarks as the flagman at the beginning of a construction zone. Although you have a signal to move ahead, it simply isn't safe or appropriate to step on the gas and speed forward. Proceed with caution and pay careful attention to the conditions around you. Your loved one's roadway may be littered with potholes or filled with treacherous debris. Soften your tone of voice, and ask questions that will lead to further discussion. Try to gain a clear understanding of what the person thinks and feels right now, and honor those feelings for what they are without trying to impose any changes. Choose your words carefully and make sure to come across as nonthreatening. At all costs, avoid pat answers and "churchy" language, as those are probably the very things your loved one has objected to in the past. Ask God to give you a gentle demeanor and help you recognize the real issues in your loved one's heart. The following are some examples of landmarks that indicate openness and possible responses to them.

- Mention of God
- Mention of fear of death/afterlife
- Reminiscing about people with strong faith
- Bringing up issues related to church—even if in anger
- Telling a joke or funny story about heaven, hell, God, angels, etc.
- "Fishing" ("How was church today?" "How is your pastor?" "Did you talk to God about me?")
- Revealing fears about God
- Asking for a member of the clergy
- Showing regret for not going to church or knowing God
- Showing regret for sin
- Other (anything is possible!)

Mention of God. Your loved one might slip God into a conversation (in a positive or negative way) that is totally out of character or context. This could even come in the form of a cliché, such as "God helps those who help themselves." Your loved one may purposely bring up this topic in order to see how you will respond. You might respond by saying something like "Do you think that is true?" "What is your opinion about that?" "I have never known how you feel about that. What do you really think?"

Mention of fear of death/afterlife. Many people have a great deal of fear about the dying process or about what happens to them after death. This is usually only revealed in a time of great vulnerability, but may be present just under the surface at other times, masked by sarcasm or false confidence. If there has been a close call and your loved one says something like "I thought I was going to die!" you could respond by asking, "What was that like for you?" Or if the doctor has brought bad news and your loved one wants to talk about it, you might be able to ask, "Are you afraid?" In this way, you voice what the person wants to say but cannot. If the person brings up this topic with sarcasm, that is also an open door. "I'm not afraid to die!" is actually a great conversation starter. A simple question like "Why is that?" may lead to an important conversation that will shed new light.

Reminiscing about people with strong faith. When your loved one says things like "My mother went to church every day," or talks about a friend (past or present) who was/is "religious," or who "prayed all the time," this shows that there has been reflection on this topic. Even getting the historical facts will help you understand whether those people were perceived as helpers or hypocrites. "What was she like?" "How old were you then?" and questions like these will yield a great deal of enlightenment for you and help you revisit this topic later.

Bringing up issues related to church—even if in anger. We all know that one of the greatest obstacles to faith is the fact that there are so many imperfect people out there who profess to have it. Your loved one may need to talk through some of these issues with you in order to come to terms with lingering frustrations or bitterness. If these come in the form of questions, try your best to answer them. But if they come in the form of indictments, accusations, or angry railings, don't feel compelled to make a defense of your fellow believers. It may be more important for your loved one to know you understand, even though you are part of "the other side." "I'm sorry that happened to you" is often an appropriate response.

Telling a joke or funny story about heaven, hell, God, angels, etc. After the laughter subsides, if there seems to be an openness, you might inquire of your loved one, "Do you think that is what it will really be like?"

"Fishing" ("How was church today?" "How is your pastor?" "Did you talk to God about me?"). Questions like these are the equivalent of spiritual flirting! Your loved one is probably trying to get the topic of God into play but is making sure it is done in a safe way. Answer the question, but then pose one of your own and see where the answer leads. Don't go too far, but come back to the topic later *("Church was great. Would you like to hear about it?" "Would you like the pastor to come see you?" "If I do talk*

to God about you, what would you like me to say?").

Revealing fears about God. Fears about God may come out blatantly, but may also be revealed through feigned aloofness. The former can be dealt with more easily and in a straightforward manner, but the latter will require more careful attention. A comment like "If I ever went to church, lightning would strike" lets you know there is some tremendous guilt that needs to be dealt with or a sin that needs to be forgiven. It might be too frightening to bring it up without a cover, but by understanding what is really being said, you can ask a direct question that will allow you to dispel the misconception.

Asking for a member of the clergy. Do not hesitate to fulfill this request, as it clearly indicates your loved one is ready for intervention. However, be sure to offer any level of assistance needed before the clergy member arrives. "Do you have a special concern?" "Can I pray for you right now, before he arrives?" "Do you know that you can pray directly to God yourself? Would you like to?"

Showing regret for not going to church or knowing God. By drawing on the story of the thief on the cross, you can reassure your loved one that it is never too late to make a decision to become right with the Lord.

Showing regret for sin. As a person comes to the end of life, there is a tendency to take an inventory of trespasses against other people. If you sense your loved one is experiencing this, do not miss the significance of it! It may be helpful for your loved one to make apologies and mend fences, and you can offer to help facilitate this by placing phone calls or inviting others to visit. On a spiritual level, this attitude of repentance is the point at which your loved one can receive Christ and experience the ultimate forgiveness.

Dad had been paralyzed from the neck down by his stroke and had been in a rehab center for three months. One day, overcome with fear that his paralysis would be permanent, he broke down in tears. This was not only a significant landmark but a wide open door. "I don't want to live like a vegetable for the rest of my life. I wish I could die," he told me through his sobs.

"Dad," I gently said, "I know it is hard being here in this hospital bed every day without being able to move. But you *aren't* a vegetable. You *are* going to die someday, and maybe God has given you a second chance to know Him before then. In the meantime, you can think, you can talk, and you can *pray*."

He responded from his brief encounters with the Catholic Church. "But I don't know any prayers." I explained he didn't need memorized prayers, but could just talk to God plainly, the way he would talk to anyone else. He was ready! So there in that hospital room, I had the unexpected joy of teaching my eighty-three-year-old father how to pray!

From that day on, Rita (Dad's wife) told me she frequently "caught" him praying when she came to visit. This was a big change for her and took her by surprise. Dad often told me with a twinkle in his eye, "I talked to the Skipper this morning!" The "Skipper" obviously heard his prayers, too, for Dad made a miraculous recovery from his stroke. He walked again—even without a cane! He knew God had healed him, and told everyone he knew what had happened. He was so grateful that for the two remaining years of his life he went to church every Sunday he was able!

KNOW WHERE YOU ARE GOING

I have spoken to many Christians who are apprehensive about talking to a dying unbeliever about the Lord. They fear deep theological questions will arise and they won't be prepared to respond. Yet in all the times I have been by the bedside of someone who was dying, no one has ever asked me about the controversy over creation versus evolution! While this may easily have been a point of contention at some other time, on the deathbed issues like this lose significance. Most often, the person is concerned with three simple things:

1. Is there really an afterlife? If yes, then . . .

2. What is God like?
3. How can I have peace with Him?

The beautiful thing is that the answer to all three of these questions is *Jesus!* Therefore, that is where the map must lead. You don't need to know debate tactics or be a theological expert. But you should know the *basics* of leading someone to Christ. (I emphasize basics because that is probably all that will be needed. Don't get sidetracked on anything else!)

Remember, long before you receive your opportunity to answer these questions, the Holy Spirit has been preparing the heart of this person. Like my friend Marge, your loved one may have already had an amazing encounter with the Lord that you know nothing about. Your words will probably only serve as confirmation for what the person has already started to believe.

Let's look at how the above questions all point to Jesus. What follows is not for your clarification as much as it is a simplified version of the Gospel that may be helpful as you share with your loved one.

Is there really an afterlife?

Answer: Yes! How do we know? *Jesus!* He died and *rose again after three days.* There is historical evidence that proves this, including numerous eyewitnesses who gave their lives to defend this fact. If His physical body did in fact die, His Spirit could not be reunited with it three days later unless there is truly an afterlife. The spirit, therefore, must live on independently of the body.

What is God like?

Answer: *Jesus!* The Bible clearly tells us that Jesus came to show us what God is like. His character, which is loving and forgiving, represents the very nature of God.

> The Son is the radiance of God's glory and the exact representation of his being.
> —HEBREWS 1:3 NIV

No one has ever seen God. But the one and only Son is himself God and is near to the Father's heart. He has revealed God to us.
—JOHN 1:18 NLT

How can I have peace with God?
Answer: *Jesus!*

For God so loved the world, that He gave His only begotten Son, that whoever believes in Him shall not perish, but have eternal life.
—JOHN 3:16

For Christ himself has made peace between us. . . . He has broken down the wall of hostility that used to separate us.
—EPHESIANS 2:14 NLT

Remember, the road on the map that leads Home is *Jesus*, and all other roads lead into the wilderness. Know the map. When the opportunity comes to share what you know, be ready to present the basic truth in a *simple*, loving way, and leave out what isn't necessary. It will be enough.

We are told that Christ was killed for us, that His death has washed out our sins, and that by dying He disabled death itself. That is the formula. That is Christianity. That is what has to be believed.
——C. S. LEWIS, *Mere Christianity*

CHAPTER 6

Sturdy Shoes
(For the Rugged Terrain)

And, as shoes for your feet . . .
put on the readiness given by the gospel of peace.
—EPHESIANS 6:15 ESV

I just returned from Yosemite National Park, where I did several all-day hikes. In preparation, I purchased a new pair of hiking shoes. Those shoes are made of excellent materials that are light, durable, completely waterproof, and able to get excellent traction. Best of all, they are amazingly comfortable, even on tough terrain. I bounded across rapid streams on slippery rocks, trekked up and down trails cut into sheer granite, and hiked for several days in a row without ever getting a blister or losing my footing. Those shoes made all the difference.

One thing I neglected to say about my hiking shoes is that they aren't beautiful. In fact, they are downright ugly. I tried on every other pair in the store to avoid buying those hideous gray and green monstrosities, but I knew those shoes were exactly what I needed. They aren't glamorous, but they certainly get the job done.

You need sturdy shoes, too. This journey isn't a leisurely stroll, but a serious hike. Having a loved one approach death will drain you spiritually, emotionally, and physically. But if you wear the right shoes, I guarantee you will make it.

The shoes you need are not pretty in the world's eyes, but from God's vantage point, and in terms of their pure functionality, they are indeed beautiful. The King James Version of the Bible talks about being "shod with the preparation of the gospel," which means being ready to step into any role that will make it easier for the gospel to penetrate. And when someone is dying, the only shoe that will fit that job is serving. There is nothing that will melt away disbelief faster or more efficiently than plain, ordinary, utilitarian, rubber-meets-the-road serving. If any Christian has ever done a remarkable act of kindness for you, you know how true this is.

Years ago, just after moving to a new city, I had a surgery that incapacitated me for several weeks. While I was still in the hospital, a deacon from the church we had been attending called to ask when someone could bring over meals. I didn't think anyone at the church even knew me, so I was astounded! Church members faithfully brought meals and offered to run errands while I recovered. I received cards, phone calls, and flowers, all from people at the church who barely knew me. Though I was already a Christian, these gestures of kindness and faith in action made a huge impression on me. Imagine the impact on an unbeliever!

Service comes in a thousand different shapes and sizes. How you serve will depend on the personality and needs of the other person, your personality and abilities, and most of all on the leading of the Holy Spirit. There is no formula that will work for everyone. The key is to find a need and fill it.

My mother and my friend Arline went through cancer treatments at the same time. I spent as much time as I could with each of them, and was struck by how differently they dealt with illness. One needed privacy and a sense of control, while the other longed for companionship and high adventure.

My mom had a need to "run a tight ship." For her, cancer

meant she was no longer in control of her life, and that represented a crisis. Before she became ill, she had started a home remodeling project (with her own hands!). During chemo, she wasn't strong enough to do anything herself, and because of her need for privacy, she refused to hire strangers to do the work. My husband and a close friend worked doggedly every night after work on Mom's remodeling projects, and my brother, sister-in-law, and I all pitched in as often as we could. Other ways we helped her included intercepting her phone calls, because most of the time she simply didn't want to talk to anyone.

Arline, on the other hand, needed people around her. She was hospitalized for several months, and in all the times I visited her, I never—not even once—found her alone. Frequently there would be as many as ten people congregated in her room or out in the hallway as she held court from her bed. The nurses were just as charmed by Arline as her friends were, and instead of chasing away extra visitors, they rounded up chairs for everyone. The best gifts you could give Arline were your company and laughter. Both of these took her mind off her illness.

Like sturdy shoes, serving another person isn't glamorous, especially when that person is dying. This kind of serving may get downright ugly. It will take time, energy, money, and possibly even your pride. It may require you to learn new things, some of which you never wanted to know! You may get dirty and might have to hold your breath. In spite of all this, there is nothing that prepares an unbeliever's heart for the Gospel more than a Christian who shows up simply to serve. In the eyes of the recipient, the true servant is beyond beautiful.

Before you offer your help, give some careful consideration to the things that will be the most meaningful to your loved one. Keep that person's needs and style—not yours—at the forefront of your serving. Watch and listen for cues, ask questions, and try not to get your feelings hurt if something you do doesn't hit the target. Just try again. If it is hard for you to know where to begin, you might consider asking someone else who knows the person well to help you brainstorm. You can also refer again to the questions at the end of chapter 3, or if you have time, read a book on personality types and how to interact with them (see the appendix).

Remember, things that will make the most difference to the other person might seem very small to you. When I was in the hospital, and hadn't eaten for over two weeks, the first thing I was served after being cleared to eat was green Jell-O. I hate green Jell-O! I was so hungry, so sick, and so frustrated, that when I was served green Jell-O, the tears began to flow. My sister-in-law, who works in a hospital, was there with me and asked what I would rather have. (She knew there are ways to work the system.) "Red Jell-O," I whimpered. I hadn't realized there was a trade-in option, but to my amazement, she was able to procure a bowl of red Jell-O in no time at all. Though it seems silly now, at the time it was something really important. My sister-in-law suddenly became a hero to me.

That Jell-O incident also taught me that it is okay to ask for things from doctors, nurses, and hospital staff. I put this knowledge to good use when my parents were sick. For example, once when Rita was in the hospital, she wanted to take a shower, but no one was there to help her. I started asking around and procured towels, soap, shampoo, toothpaste, a comb, a fresh gown, and a nurse to disconnect the IV. The task took less than ten minutes, but changed how Rita saw me because I had proven myself to be an advocate for her. Because it is so much easier to ask on behalf of another person than for yourself, becoming an advocate in medical situations is a wonderful way to help your loved one.

There is no better model for serving than Jesus, who humbled himself and took on human form so that we could experience Him in a way that would be meaningful and understandable to us. He even summarized His own ministry by stating this concept:

The Son of Man did not come to be served, but to serve,
and to give His life a ransom for many.
—MATTHEW 20:28

As you serve a person who is dying, you not only honor Christ by following His example, but you help prepare a heart to receive the Gospel. Just like sturdy shoes, serving doesn't appear glamorous, but if you are serious about wanting to walk someone Home, serving is exactly what will take you there. Your sacrifice will become a beacon of light and hope and will help you arrive at the destination without slipping.

CHAPTER 7

GPS
(To Keep You on Track)

*Trust in the Lord with all your heart, and lean not on
your own understanding; in all your ways acknowledge
Him, and He shall direct your paths.*

—PROVERBS 3:5–6 NKJV

I prefer to buy used cars. The car I currently drive is one I
found on the Internet, and was a real bargain. It had only twenty
thousand miles on it, was less than a year old, had all the bells
and whistles I wanted, and was about half the price of the new
version. I had already made the deal and was driving the car
home when I realized it had a Global Positioning System (GPS).
An onboard computer in constant communication with a satel-
lite detects my exact location and graphically and verbally
directs me with turn-by-turn instructions. All I have to do is program in the address or phone number of where I want to go, and
the GPS does the rest! It warns me about tricky interchanges
where I can make wrong turns and helps me turn around if I go
off route. It even shows me the logos of nearby gas stations

wherever I am. As long as I pay attention to the GPS, I can never get lost or run out of gas.

Isn't it great to know that God's Positioning System is far more reliable than even the most high-tech invention man can design? He knows exactly where you are at all times. He sees all the obstacles and the tricky places in the road ahead, and is poised to give you step-by-step, turn-by-turn directions to keep you on track. He also knows where all the fueling stations are and will bring them to your attention. You have to know when your tank is getting low, but He will show you where to fill up when you are empty. He provides a direct connection with Him at all times, and even if you make a mistake, He will show you how to get back on track.

When someone you love is ill, it feels like you are in uncharted territory. There are so many unfamiliar roads and unmarked hazards as you deal with medical issues and emotional issues that may be completely new. On top of everything else, you are part of an intense spiritual battle over your loved one's soul. When you feel completely lost and don't know what to do, you must rely on God's Positioning System.

The Lord is not going to leave you alone while you are doing this work. His Holy Spirit is going to guide you, care for you, love you, and even coach you. Even though you feel stretched far past normal limits, He is with you every step of the way. Some of His instructions may not seem clear until later, but in the meantime, trust Him and know His leading is accurate.

God will guide you in several significant areas. He will show you how to serve your loved one in a meaningful way. He will give you wisdom regarding medical issues (if that is part of your role) and will provide the discernment you need for sharing your faith. He will also help you take care of yourself during this stressful time. His leading may come through prayer, through reading the Bible or a Christian book, through another believer, or through journaling. As long as you are open to what He has to say, God will find the most amazing and creative ways to communicate with you during this time when you need His guidance so much.

My mother lived across the street from us during the last four months of her life. This was a tremendous blessing in many ways because she could maintain her independence, but my husband or I could immediately be at her side to help her if necessary. However, those last months became very difficult, and I became discouraged about her spiritual condition, which didn't seem to be changing. One night I woke up about 3:00 A.M. and couldn't get back to sleep. I suddenly felt the urge to go across the street to see her. Though I wasn't sure how I would explain my late night visit, I decided to risk it.

As I quietly crept through her front door, she called out to me, indicating she had been wide awake. "What are you doing here?" she questioned, amused. By then, Mom was having trouble eating, and the only thing that ever enticed her was ice cream. "Oh, I just felt like having some ice cream," I said. She shot up from the bed and said with a giggle, "I was just lying here thinking about ice cream!" We went into the kitchen and I got out two bowls and a half gallon of pecan praline. We sat at her kitchen table for a long time enjoying our ice cream and talking. Amazingly, that was the first time she opened up to me about her fear of dying, about unfinished business she wanted to settle, and about God. The Holy Spirit knew she was ready and woke me up to send me to see her. That visit is one of the most precious memories I have of my mother.

God's Positioning System, the Holy Spirit, will give you turn-by-turn directions. Meanwhile, Jesus is at the right hand of the Father interceding for you. You can't go wrong.

For this is God, our God forever and ever; He will be our guide even to death.
—PSALM 48:14 NKJV

CHAPTER 8

Emergency Information
(The Documents You Will Need)

The palest ink is better than the best memory.
—CHINESE PROVERB

One of my favorite ways to be alone with God is walking or riding my bike. The combination of being outside, moving, and praying at the same time is spiritually restorative and physically invigorating. While I am by no means an athlete, I am in decent shape and can be gone for hours on these little mini-retreats. Only recently has it occurred to me that I need to start taking safety precautions, such as bringing a cell phone, identification, and emergency contact information when I venture away from my neighborhood alone. Though I am not anticipating an emergency, if one occurred, I would want things to go as smoothly as possible.

While walking alongside someone who is terminally ill, you should also take precautions. There may never be a dramatic emergency, but if there is, you can greatly improve the outcome by taking a few preliminary measures, such as making sure all documents are in order. Gathering information before it is needed will greatly reduce stress—both for you and your loved one—and will reduce the time it will take for intervention. If others will help provide care for your loved one, having emergency information readily available will also empower them to take action as quickly as necessary.

BASIC INFORMATION

Most of us do not think as clearly during an emergency as at other times. And the ongoing stress of having a loved one who is ill is extremely wearing, which can also affect our ability to recall information we would normally readily know. This became clear to me once when I had to call my mother's insurance company during a very stressful health crisis. In order to verify coverage, I was asked to give her date of birth. Because I had been handling her health care issues for months, I was giving out this same information on practically a daily basis, and of course had it memorized. However, at that moment my mind went completely blank. The representative, who was just following proper procedures, would not answer any of my questions until I was able to look the date up and relay it to her. This not only wasted precious time but it also increased my already high level of anxiety.

Shortly after that incident, I created a notebook that contained everything relating to my mother's health situation. On the inside cover where it was immediately visible, I wrote her date of birth, insurance card number, and doctor's phone number in large print. Using notebook dividers, I made clearly marked sections to list medications, medical providers, and track changes in blood work and temperature. Legal documents had their own section, as did insurance records. The notebook became an indispensable tool for our entire family, including my mother, who used it as much as any of us. It was kept next to the phone, and even neighbors knew where to find it if needed. The notebook also went along on several hospital visits, allowing us to verify names and dosages of medications that were being taken. This method so simplified our lives that later, when my stepmother and father became ill, we created similar notebooks for them, too.

Whether kept in a well-organized notebook or a file folder, it is essential to keep important health-related information in one designated place. Depending on your situation, it may also be advisable to have a second set of records in the safekeeping of an additional family member. If your loved one is still quite active and frequently out of the house, it is also wise to tuck a listing of medical conditions and medications taken (including dosages) inside his or her purse or wallet to make it accessible in unforeseen circumstances.

DOCUMENTS THAT EMPOWER

To ensure your loved one's wishes will be followed if a serious medical emergency occurs, it is necessary to have several legal documents in place. Without these written directives, important life-and-death decisions will be left in the hands of a physician who may not even know your loved one. Even though they require almost no time or monetary investment to prepare, these documents are often not completed because they relate to issues that are sometimes uncomfortable or difficult to discuss. However, the very best time to put these directives in place is before they are needed. Entering a health crisis without them can be devastating. When these documents are in order, your loved one and all involved (including you) will be much more empowered to face any medical situation that may occur. The various types of documents needed, as well as their advantages and disadvantages, are discussed below.

Living Will

Many people erroneously believe a living will is sufficient to ensure that their wishes for end-of-life care will be carried out. However, there are serious limitations to this type of document. Living wills tend to be vague and do not always clearly indicate which measures should be taken or avoided. Instead, a doctor who does not necessarily know the patient is given full authority to make decisions whether to withhold or withdraw treatment. Living wills generally apply only to situations of terminal illness and do not cover other emergencies, especially of a temporary nature. Because they do not clearly define "treatment," living wills may therefore be interpreted to include hydration and nutrition as treatment rather than standard care. For these reasons, it is important for your loved one to have more specific written instructions about end-of-life care.

Advance Health Care Directive

The advance health care directive is preferable to the living will and provides much more specific information. It is called "advance" because it is prepared *before* health care decisions must be made, and is called "directive" because it clearly states who will speak on behalf of the person and precisely what kind of treatments should or should not be done. This document can be prepared by an attorney, or by filling in forms provided by a doctor or hospital staff member. The advance directive has several parts, each described below.

Durable Power of Attorney for Health Care Decisions (DPAHCD). This document designates someone to act on behalf of your loved one as a legal surrogate or agent regarding medical issues. The designated person, usually a relative or close friend, makes choices regarding care if the person becomes incapacitated, or if specified, even earlier. A "second," or alternate, agent is usually named in case the first designee is unavailable during an emergency.

Individual Health Care Instruction. A written individual health care instruction states your loved one's wishes about interventions, such as ventilators, feeding tubes, resuscitation, and other treatment options. By using this document, your loved one may clearly specify which treatments are desired and under what circumstances. Though the Individual Health Care Instruction may specifically exclude certain treatment options, it may be changed or updated at any time.

Do-Not-Resuscitate (DNR) Order. This document indicates the patient does not want "heroic" or aggressive measures taken in a life-threatening situation. The interventions generally excluded are cardiopulmonary resuscitation (CPR), defibrillators, and/or ventilators. Terminally ill patients often choose to have a DNR order on file, as they do not want to be kept alive artificially, and many hospices routinely use this form during the intake process.

Although discussing these issues may initially be awkward, remember to reassure your loved one that these documents will ensure that his or her wishes for end-of-life care will be honored, and will protect those faced with making difficult decisions from feeling uncertain about what to do in an emergency.

Special Circumstances

What happens if your loved one has second thoughts about a treatment option, or an emergency arises that was not discussed? If your loved one or anyone else calls 9-1-1, emergency health care workers will take all possible intervention measures, even if this contradicts a written directive. Likewise, unless instructed otherwise, hospital staff will take every measure to save life.

When my father went on hospice, he specified no heroic measures should be taken if he stopped breathing. All the appropriate papers were signed and included in his emergency notebook. One night while I was staying with him, his nose began to bleed. He was taking blood thinners at the time and frequently had nosebleeds, so at first, I wasn't alarmed. However, after twenty minutes, he was having serious trouble breathing. "Call 9-1-1!" he managed to say. Shortly afterward, paramedics arrived and rushed him to the hospital. I followed the ambulance in my car, oblivious to the serious danger my father was facing.

The ER doctor took me aside and in hushed tones asked whether a DNR order was in place. It took a moment for the implication to register. I thought my father had a simple nose-bleed, and I had not understood he was at the crossroads of life and death. Suddenly I was faced with the decision of whether heroic measures should be taken, or if it was time to let my father die.

My mind raced into high gear. I knew Dad did in fact have a DNR order and had told us not to intervene if he stopped breathing. But this was different. When the bleeding started, he was fully conscious and had called out for help. Even now, he was wide awake, drowning in his own blood. I had every indication he wanted to live, so I told the doctor to insert the breathing tube.

Having the DNR order in place did not prevent me from making the decision for medical intervention. Because this specific situation had not been anticipated, I wasn't exactly sure what to do, but I made the best decision I could based on the information I had. My father recovered from that incident after only a few days with the tube in place, and I felt relieved I had acted as I did.

Other Documents

This chapter has focused mainly on how to prepare for a medical emergency. Of course, it is also important for your loved one to have a will or trust that specifies how assets and possessions are to be distributed after death. If your loved one already has a will or trust in place, be sure it is current. If it needs to be updated, or if one has never been prepared, contact an experienced attorney who specializes in estate planning and fully understands tax matters. The investment in legal fees will be well worth the assurance that this important matter has been dealt with properly. If the fees seem prohibitive, look for an organization that provides low-cost legal assistance (see the appendix).

Just as the Durable Power of Attorney for Health Care Decisions appoints a legal surrogate to make *medical* decisions for someone, a Durable Power of Attorney for Financial Decisions appoints a surrogate for other legal matters. These representatives do not need to be the same person. Likewise, someone may be appointed to deal with immediate financial decisions, but a different person may be appointed to handle the estate. For instance, I was designated to deal with my mother's medical care and was listed on her bank accounts so I could help her pay her bills. However, after she died, my brother served as the executor of the estate. This arrangement worked extremely well for us, because the load was evenly distributed between my brother and me, and allowed each of us to act in our particular area of strength.

In summary, the issues discussed in this chapter may initially be uncomfortable to discuss with your loved one, but doing so will prevent the unnecessary stress of trying to make hasty, uninformed decisions or leaving those decisions to others. Any initial discomfort will be far outweighed by the relief and empowerment that are the result of putting procedures and guidelines into place before they are needed.

CHAPTER 9

Traveler's Assistance
(When You Feel Lost and Weary)

In everyone's life, at some time, our inner fire goes out.
It is then burst into flame by an encounter with
another human being. We should all be thankful for
those people who rekindle our inner spirit.
—ALBERT SCHWEITZER

In 1992, while I was still working as an opera singer, I went to Germany to audition for several of the state opera houses there. East and West Germany had just been reunified, and the eastern half of the country still had a few kinks that had not yet been worked out. In West Germany, the trains were so punctual you could set your watch by them. Though I didn't yet know it, in the East there was only a 50 percent chance the train would arrive at all.

After one audition in a small burg a few hours north of Berlin, I got stranded in the train station. My German was good enough to be functional in the West (where almost everyone spoke fluent English!) but was too spotty to get by in the East, where only perfect German or Russian would suffice. I had been waiting for trains all night, going from one platform to the next looking for the trains listed on the schedule, but none were materializing. At first, I wondered if I had made a mistake or was reading a schedule from another station. Soon I realized something was terribly wrong. I mentally replayed old World War II movies with the heroine caught in Berlin, behind enemy lines. Maybe I would never get out alive! I was tired, frightened, and totally alone in a foreign city where I couldn't communicate. It was long past midnight, and I had no idea how to get home or even find a hotel. I needed help!

After some frantic searching, I finally found a small window with a sign indicating Traveler's Assistance was provided. A young man who spoke English appeared and explained that in East Germany, the train schedule was merely a wish list for when travelers might *like* the trains to run. Trains were late all the time, so no need for alarm! He thought that in just two more hours another train would actually arrive, headed for Frankfurt. I'm sure he knew I had been crying, and he kindly offered me a mouth-watering piece of chocolate, just for comfort. When the whole ordeal was over, I wondered, "Why didn't I get help sooner?"

CALL FOR HELP

When you are walking alongside someone who is dying, you, too, may need "traveler's assistance." You may be reluctant to ask for help, but it is important for you to get help as soon as you realize you need it. Don't waste precious time trying to do things completely on your own. Instead, find out where the help is and let people know you need it. That is the *only way* to get through this. If possible, put some contingency plans in place before you need them. If I had seen the Traveler's Assistance window right away, I could have used my energies positively rather than panicking. In this chapter, we will look at some of the various kinds of traveler's assistance that are available for your journey, the benefits you will receive from utilizing them, and where you can find these services.

YOUR PERSONAL SUPPORT TEAM

My next-door neighbor is a dietitian for a local hospice. She and her colleagues work with the terminally ill on a daily basis and are accustomed to death. Even so, every week they attend mandatory meetings—not only to discuss patient needs but also to deal with the effects of grief.

If seasoned professionals need help coping with death, how much more must the rest of us need assistance! There is nothing more challenging than facing the loss of a loved one, and the closer you are to the person, the more difficult it will be. If you are also providing care, your level of stress will rise exponentially. You are going to need support.

I believe it is best to have a support *team*, because no one person will be able to help with everything you will need. The person who is willing to pick up your kids from school might not be the same person you would call in the middle of the night if there is a life-and-death emergency and you need prayer. Both of these people will be very important to you, but will serve in completely different capacities.

When my mother was dying, I had a huge support team made up of people who each helped in their own unique way. For the most part, their roles didn't overlap, but together they made sure I was able to keep moving toward the goal. Here are some of the people on that team:

Robin—cried with me
Carole—prayed with me
Louise—talked it out with me
Kelly—encouraged me; repeatedly told me I was doing a good job
Pride—loved me; was a true helpmeet in every way
Kristy—let me complain without judging me; helped provide care

Stan—attended to all nonmedical legal matters
Vernie—provided respite care and spiritual support
Eula—met me at the hospital for every ER visit; prayed
    behind the scenes
Jeff, Sherri, Juan, Sam, Al, Betty, John, Marilyn, and dea-
    cons—abundantly provided the gift of helps
Allison—told me what to expect next

You may not need as big a support team as I did, but try to name two or three key people who will be willing to help you or lend you moral support while you go through this. The following checklist will help. Next to each category, write the name of a person who is already helping you or who would be willing to assist in that specific area of support. Pray about the person joining your support team and about the right time to talk with him or her about it.

Some people will miraculously wind up on your support team without your even asking. They will stand with you in ways you could never have asked for or predicted. Conversely, someone you might have thought would be likely to help you will not be able to do so for one reason or another. If this happens, try not to take it personally or be upset with the person. This often is simply an indicator that God has someone else in mind for you! If you focus on your disappointment, you will become in-effective, and you can't afford that distraction right now.

MY PERSONAL SUPPORT TEAM

1. My prayer support person: _____

2. The person I can call in the middle of the night: _____

3. A person who might run an errand: _____

4. The person to talk to when I am really low: _____

5. A person who will come sit with me: _____

6. A person who has already been through this: _____

7. Someone I know with a medical background: _____

8. My church prayer-chain contact: _____

9. My fun, get-away-from-it-all person: _____

10. The person who will cry with me: _____

By thinking about who these people are now, you will be much more comfortable asking for help later. If you are reluctant, remember that one of the most satisfying experiences a person can have is to minister to someone else. Don't cheat your friends and brothers and sisters in Christ of their chance to be blessed and be a blessing!

HELP AWAY FROM HOME

If the person who is dying lives far away and you must travel to another city to be with him or her, you may need to remain in close contact with your support team while you are away. Some creative ways of maintaining contact are listed below.

Phone Calls

The cost of a call you make to someone on your support team can be a very wise investment, so this is not the time to worry about long-distance charges. How often do you go through a life-and-death situation? Because you're trying to love someone into the kingdom, and are dealing with matters of eternal importance, you may need constant prayer and encouragement. Therefore, remain in communication with those who can help lift your spirits and keep you focused. By following some basic guidelines, you can still do this very cost effectively.

- Make your conversations brief. It's better just to call and say, "I need prayer!" than not to call at all.
- Pass the word. Let each member of your team know the names and contact information of the others. Call one person on the team and ask him or her to call the others. If your

team is large, ask each person to call the next person on the list so each only makes one additional phone call. It will be like having your own prayer chain!

- Purchase a phone card before you leave home.
- Change your cell phone plan to one that has nationwide long distance. Be sure to check with your provider, because some plans charge extra fees for changes made in the middle of the billing cycle.
- Look into low-cost or even free Internet-based phone services.

The Internet

An easy and inexpensive way to stay in touch with the people on your support team is through the Internet. If your destination doesn't have a computer but you have a laptop, consider bringing it with you. If not, your loved one may have a neighbor who will be willing to provide you with Internet access.

1. E-mail your support team about medical developments, prayer needs, and concerns.
2. Arrange for a chat or instant messaging (IM) on the computer with members of your support team at a designated time.
3. Utilize Internet-based phone services.

YOUR CHURCH

In addition to the sustenance provided by your inner circle of close friends, you will need the kind of support that comes from the body of Christ in general. Your pastor and friends from church may already be part of your personal support team, but if not, be sure to communicate with them about what is happening. Contact the church prayer chain or key prayer warriors and emphasize the spiritual need of your loved one. Ask them to pray continually, and keep them updated about changes that occur.

If you must travel to a faraway city, it may be helpful to connect with a pastor or an elder from a church near your loved one. This will prevent you from feeling isolated and may also lead to another spiritual contact for your loved one, as pastors are often willing to make home or hospital visits even to those outside their congregation (initiate this only if your loved one is open to it). Having a pastoral ally in the community will also be an asset when you are ready to plan a funeral or memorial service.

Stephen Ministries

Some churches have Stephen Ministers, deacons, or similar lay-leaders who help families in crisis by providing one-on-one lay counseling, or who will prepare meals, provide transportation, or assist with other practical matters. Although these groups are ready to help, they can't respond unless they know of your need. Don't wait for them to contact you. Instead, actively seek out any available resources your church may offer. Find out which services exist and utilize them as soon as possible.

MEALS ON WHEELS

Most cities have Meals on Wheels for the elderly or those housebound by illness. The phone number is usually available in the white pages of the phone book or through Directory Assistance. The local hospital community services department or a nearby community senior center will also be able to refer you to these services. Most metropolitan area Meals on Wheels services operate their own Web sites, so if you are checking on the Internet, simply do a search for *Meals on Wheels* to find your local point of contact.

SUPPORT GROUPS

Every hospital offers classes and support groups free of charge to members of the community. Both you and your loved one can benefit from these classes as topics include caregiving, grief, cancer support, heart attack recovery, and other related subjects. Classes may be weekly, biweekly, or monthly, and provide a forum where those who are going through similar experiences can come together to learn or offer valuable insights to one another.

Support groups for caregivers can be very helpful as they help keep the challenges of this monumental job in perspective. They also provide an outlet to talk to others who understand and can give you a periodic "reality check." Grief support is extremely important, even before your loved one passes away. My friend Naomi cared for her dying husband for several years. Realizing she was already beginning the grieving process, she joined a grief group while her husband was still alive. The information she gained was extremely helpful in preparing to let go, and helped her prepare her three young daughters for that process, too.

While my mother was going through cancer treatments she became extremely discouraged, as is understandable. Though she was not typically interested in social gatherings, I wondered whether she might be interested in attending a cancer support group. I called the hospital, was given the name and phone number of the group leader, and called to inquire about details. A friendly woman who identified herself as a cancer survivor described the class and even offered to provide transportation if my mother decided to attend. To my delight, Mom agreed to give the class a try. The group became an important part of her life, and she raved about the benefits of watching others whose situations were far worse than her own overcome the obstacles cancer presented. The group was an amazing source of encouragement for my mother and helped her to stay focused on the positive aspects of her life during her struggle with cancer.

The best sources for support groups are local hospitals, hospice agencies, the American Cancer Society (or similar organizations specializing in other diseases), the local wellness center, or private therapists. Support groups are almost always free of charge, and the benefits are immeasurable. For more information about where to find support groups, see the appendix.

SPECIAL AGENCIES

One of the best ways to find help is to contact one of the special agencies that deals with health-related issues. For instance, the American Cancer Society provides a wide variety of services for patients and their families. With local chapters in almost every part of the country, the ACS is readily accessible and can provide printed information about specific types of cancer, loan chests to help supply wheelchairs and wigs, volunteers who help provide transportation to and from treatments, and a doctor referral program. There are similar groups for every disease imaginable, including rare ones. For specific listings, refer to the appendix.

THE SOCIAL WORKER

I used to think a social worker was someone who worked with abused children and helped place them in foster homes. Only when my parents became ill did I learn that hospitals and hospices have social workers who specialize in end-of-life issues. These professionals act as intermediaries, provide links to important services, and also offer emotional support. The social worker will be the champion for your loved one and will help you find the resources you need to keep going. I cannot overemphasize the importance of having one on your team.

Hospital Social Workers

Hospital social workers are available to any admitted or recently released patient. However, due to limited resources, the social worker is not *automatically* sent unless the situation is dire. Otherwise, a request must be made. Generally a doctor or nurse must make the connection, but either you or your loved one may initiate this process.

The social worker can:

1. Inform you of available services or support groups that may be of benefit to the patient or family members.
2. Help provide and complete important documents, such as Durable Power of Attorney for Health Care Decisions and do-not-resuscitate (DNR) order.
3. Be present to help break difficult news.
4. Help talk to the patient and/or family members about hospice.
5. Provide emotional care for you or your loved one.
6. Connect you to resources in the community.

Hospice Social Workers

Hospice, which differs from traditional care (see following section), also employs social workers. Generally a visit from a social worker is a *routine* part of the hospice enrollment process, and the social worker is readily available to each patient.

At the time of her diagnosis my mother had inoperable stage-four (the most progressed) cancer. I had done some homework and knew she probably would not survive even a year. However, she did not want to know her prognosis because she thought it would interfere with her ability to fight the disease. Initially, this was positive, but as her illness progressed and she began to lose that battle, practical decisions had to be made about her estate and final arrangements. Her resistance made it impossible to talk about these things. I was at a complete loss about what to do.

Our hospice agency arranged for a visit from the social worker. As the three of us chatted comfortably over coffee, I realized I was watching a master at work! The social worker had a low-key, non-threatening approach, much different from my blunt, get-to-the-bottom-line style. She spoke in general, hypothetical terms about funeral arrangements, and used phrases like *"someday, if the need should ever arise,"* and *"for instance, when someone. . . ."* She never talked specifically about *my mother's* funeral, but still managed to find out her preferences for disposition of remains and service arrangements. Most important, the social worker left my mother's hope and will to fight completely intact, whereas I might have attempted to force Mom to face the bitter truth. That visit provided a huge relief for me and accomplished something I could not have done without assistance.

HOSPICE CARE

Of all the resources available for the dying, hospice care is by far the most important. All three of my parents received hospice care and died at home, and I would highly recommend that anyone with a terminal illness consider this option. My only regret about hospice is not calling them sooner.

Hospice care is often misunderstood. Many people think hospice is a *place* you go, or that it is a service for only the very last few days of life. Due to these misconceptions, people are sometimes afraid of hospice. Because they think it is the equivalent of giving up hope, they miss out on the tremendous help they could receive.

Hospice is an interdisciplinary team approach to end-of-life care. It provides service in the patient's own home or long-term care facility. The main difference between hospice and traditional care is in philosophy. In the hospital, doctors and nurses try to find the source of symptoms and aggressively look for curative methods of dealing with them, often with highly invasive procedures and heroic measures. In contrast, hospice provides palliative, or *comfort* care, and focuses on symptom management. Hospice helps the patient remain in control of treatment and enables them to remain in familiar surroundings through to the end.

Patients who have grown weary of tests, surgeries, and endless procedures often view hospice as a welcome relief. Likewise, family members who are already drained from providing care for a loved one may receive so much support from the hospice team that they will feel as though the cavalry has arrived to save the fort!

Because hospice is a holistic approach to care, it provides comprehensive services, such as:

1. Physician
2. Nurse
3. Social worker
4. Chaplain
5. Dietitian
6. Certified hospice health aide to assist with bathing and personal needs
7. Volunteers
8. Durable medical equipment (delivered to the home)
9. Medications delivered (if related to hospice diagnosis)
10. 24-hour nursing hotline
11. Emotional, mental, and spiritual support for patient and family members
12. Respite care
13. Bereavement support

For the eleven months of my mother's battle with cancer, I was her primary caregiver. At first, I raced back and forth across Southern California from my city to hers so that I could be with her as much as possible and still retain some semblance of my usual routine. Later, when she moved into a house right across the street from us, logistics became much easier but her declining condition brought new concerns on a daily basis. Caring for her was a tremendous privilege, and was something I wanted to do, but still it was extremely draining and often left me emotionally and physically exhausted. There were so many decisions that had to be made, and because I didn't have a medical background, they felt like uncharted territory to me. All the while I was dealing with my own emotional upheaval at the thought of losing my mother and trying to tend to her needs at the same time. There were times when I felt as though I were stranded all alone in a blinding blizzard, carrying a huge load up an enormous mountainside without a trail to mark my way. When my mother went on hospice, there was a flurry of activity centered around her needs. However, I benefited, as well. I suddenly felt as though an entire search-and-rescue team had emerged out of nowhere, rallied to my side, and brought me to safety. It was still snowing, but I was no longer stranded. The support offered by hospice immediately brought me new hope, resources, and resolve.

The main point of contact in hospice care is the nurse. Though a doctor may initially examine the patient, the nurse is the one who monitors progress, recommends changes in medication, and calls in other team members to assist in care. The nurse also plays a vital role in empowering the caregiver and the family to deal with medical challenges and cope with the emotional demands placed on them.

Allison was Mom's hospice nurse, and she was such an angel that I still envision her wearing a halo! Allison knew right away that my mother was a "tough cookie," and as is consistent with the hospice philosophy, she let my mother be completely in charge. The frequency of Allison's visits, the tasks she performed, and the medications were all discussed with, scrutinized, and approved by my mom. If she didn't want to be "pestered" with having her vital signs taken, Allison didn't take them. If she didn't want to take any medication, she didn't have to. For someone who is continually fighting a losing battle with health and life, having even a small measure of control is extremely satisfying and empowering. Allison's approach had a tremendously positive effect on my mother's attitude. Having treatment in your own home is completely different than being rushed to an emergency room to be poked and prodded by doctors who have never met you. Allison became a friend, and all of us looked forward to her visits.

For me, the role that Allison played was very different. She became a mentor for me and prepared me for what was coming. It wasn't until after my mother died that I fully understood how brilliant Allison had been in carrying out this part of her job. She never gave me information I didn't yet need, but briefed me fully on whatever situation was brewing at the time. She always made it abundantly clear that I could call the hospice hotline at any time of the day or night, and if needed, she would come immediately. When my mother was having a bad day—either physically or emotionally—Allison would always tend to her, make sure she was comfortably tucked in bed, and then make time to sit and talk with me about all the ramifications of what was happening. As we came closer and closer to the end of Mom's struggle, Allison led me through the process. As a result, I was never surprised by the changes I saw and never felt panicked. In this way, Allison helped both my mother and me retain a degree of being in control during what was a fairly out-of-control situation.

Allison told us she attended church, but her personal beliefs never emerged as a central point in her relationship with us. This may have been because she sensed that my mother was not particularly faith-focused and wanted to honor her feelings. Allison did, however, make a referral to the hospice chaplain, who visited with my mother. Though each nurse and patient relationship is unique, spiritual care of hospice patients is usually delegated to one of the chaplains who is part of the hospice team.

Hospice Requirements

Generally, a doctor referral is a prerequisite for hospice care. However, it is *not* necessary to wait for the physician to bring up this option! Doctors sometimes prefer that the patient lead in this area and may be reluctant to suggest hospice due to the inherent implications. And not every doctor agrees with the philosophy of hospice. If you or your loved one would like to explore this option, but the doctor seems uninformed or resistant, it is perfectly permissible to obtain the name of a local hospice agency and ask a representative to visit and explain hospice care. The hospice physician may then make the referral, if appropriate.

Some hospice programs will want to know if a family member or friend will be available to serve as a caregiver if the patient cannot be left alone. If no one is available and this presents a safety issue, hospice may require the patient to enter a skilled nursing facility. Hospice patients in such a setting will receive more comprehensive care due to the added benefits available. The only other requirement for hospice is a terminal condition. Generally hospice is available to anyone with a prognosis of six months or less, but because illness is unpredictable, patients often remain on hospice for much longer periods. One dear woman I knew had hospice care for more than three years! Patients who improve are generally discharged to traditional care, while those who continue to decline, no matter the length of time, remain on hospice.

Who Pays for Hospice?

Hospice is almost always paid for by Medicare, as long as the hospice is Medicare-approved. As the transition to hospice is made, you or your loved one will be connected to those who can help determine benefits eligibility. A representative from your insurance company, the hospice, or Medicare will then answer your specific questions.

Some private insurance plans require patients to go on hospice for ninety- or sixty-day intervals that may be renewed as needed. If your loved one improves during that time and no longer needs hospice, the return to traditional care is very easy. (My father, nicknamed "Energizer Bunny," because of his ability to bounce back, went back and forth between traditional care and hospice three times!)

RESPITE CARE

If you or another family member will be providing care to your loved one, you should have a plan for respite care. Respite care provides a break, or *respite*, from the grueling physical and emotional demands of caring for the terminally ill. A person who is dying often requires the same level of care as an infant, needing to be fed, bathed, and even changed, leaving caregivers exhausted or even depressed. Obtaining occasional relief is important for emotional, physical, and spiritual health.

If a relative or friend offers to help, graciously accept! Caregivers often are reluctant to "burden someone else" and burn themselves out by being too stoic. Even a few hours away will provide a new perspective, but if the illness will be long term, longer periods (a weekend, perhaps) will offer the deep refreshment that is needed to carry on for the long haul.

Caregivers must remember, too, that not everyone will be able to help. This can feel extremely disappointing, and can cause tension or resentment toward others who seem to shirk responsibility or be oblivious to the weariness of the caregiver. However, for the Christian, the opportunity to serve a dying unbeliever is also an incredible opportunity to see God in action. Though carrying a heavy load, the caregiver is also the most likely person to observe the miraculous and be able to win the person to Christ. Keeping this perspective will help.

Insurance or Medicare sometimes pays for nonmedical home health workers who can assist with care (this is usually included in hospice care). If no insurance benefit is available and you can afford it, paying for help may be a valuable investment. Your hospice team or hospital social worker can provide names of reputable agencies that specialize in respite care. Using an agency is preferable to hiring someone independently, because the agency handles payment and acts as an intermediary if there are problems with a worker. The cost of using an agency is generally no different from hiring an individual, but the protection is much greater.

Many hospice agencies will provide up to five days of respite care for family members who need to get away. While this is an invaluable service, it is often dependent on your loved one entering a skilled nursing facility while the caregiver is away. Be sure to check with your hospice facility for details.

One final word about respite care: If you are not a primary caregiver, but you are involved with someone who is, *please* consider offering a measure of relief to that person. There is no other role in life that is so exhausting, and the demands are incomprehensible to those who have not served in this capacity. Even if you don't know how to help, ask. Your assistance may be what keeps the caregiver going, and the love and kindness you show will not soon be forgotten.

PART THREE

No Turning Back

CHAPTER 10

Spiritual Warfare

*For our struggle is not against flesh and blood, but against
the rulers, against the powers, against the world forces
of this darkness, against the spiritual forces of
wickedness in the heavenly places.*
—Ephesians 6:12

Whenever any Christian endeavors to win a soul to Christ,
there is intense spiritual warfare taking place to prevent it. Just
as all the angels in heaven rejoice over one sinner who repents
(Luke 15:10), all the demons of hell rejoice over one sinner who
is lost to God forever. Therefore, the bad news is that as you
reach out to your dying loved one, you are fighting a war against
the devil and all his forces. But the good news is that God and
the hosts of heaven are on your side, and they are far more powerful than the opponent.

This may be the most important mission of your life. God has
sent you on a special operation to go behind enemy lines, storm
the prison, and bring the hostage all the way to safety. This task
is difficult, with many inherent risks and dangers. Not only must

you consider the prisoner's welfare but you must also keep yourself out of harm's way. Fortunately, your Commanding Officer has carefully planned this operation and will be in constant communication with you. Even so, the opponent is cunning and must not be taken lightly. He doesn't fight fairly and is ready and willing to use any tactic to keep your loved one out of heaven. Keeping this in mind, ask yourself the following questions:

1. What is God trying to accomplish right now?
2. Would Satan have any reason to interfere?
3. Are things going wrong for no apparent reason?
4. Are events in my life taking my eyes off of God or His purposes?
5. Am I trying to change something I can't change on my own?
6. Am I treating a situation or person as the enemy?
7. Am I deeply discouraged or depressed, even though there are things to be thankful for?
8. Does the situation around me seem impossible?
9. Do I feel cut off from God?
10. Do I feel hopeless?

If you answered yes to more than three of these questions, you are probably under spiritual attack. But don't despair, this is wonderful news! Your mission is so important, Satan has taken notice of it! He knows that by distracting and discouraging you, he can keep your loved one's soul lost forever. However, he may have forgotten the power of his opponent: "The Spirit who lives in you is greater than the spirit who lives in the world" (1 John 4:4 NLT).

COUNT YOUR BLESSINGS

Once you realize you are under attack, take stock of your situation with different eyes. How is the Lord proving himself faithful to you? What are the signs of progress you can see? How has Christ ministered to you? Have you learned any valuable lessons? What are the things from your past that have already prepared you for this moment? You may want to write these down and keep them nearby as reminders. Begin to praise the Lord and thank Him for all He has done and will do. This will not only strengthen and encourage you but it is also a mighty force against the enemy. Remember the scene in *The Wizard of Oz* where the Wicked Witch melts? This is the effect on Satan when we offer praise and thanksgiving to God!

THE FATHER OF LIES

Satan is a thief, a murderer, and a liar. Jesus, who had firsthand experience wrestling against this enemy, called Satan the father of lies (John 8:44). His lies are one of his greatest weapons, and he will use them to discourage you and take your hope away. The only way to fight him is with the truth, which is exactly what Jesus did. First, recognize the lie, then speak the truth—especially biblical truth—that addresses the falsehood:

- It **feels** hopeless, but the **truth** is, nothing is impossible with God.
- My mother **might** only have a few weeks to live. The **truth** is, God is in control, no matter what the time frame.
- I am tired and it **seems** I can't keep going. The **truth** is, this will not last forever, and God will renew my strength.

You may have to repeatedly remind yourself of the *truth* of your situation, but this is the only way to survive against the relentless and brutal lies of the enemy. You have too much at stake to give in to his tactics.

He Divides and Conquers

Another way the enemy works is through use of the "divide and conquer" strategy. He capitalizes on the countless demands that accompany serious illness and uses them to distract attention away from the Lord. He first attempts to break off all communication, then seizes the first opportunity to separate the unsuspecting opponent from other troops and from the Commander. You must combat this technique by remaining in close contact with mature believers and by finding time to spend with God. Staying connected to those on your support team will help you keep a good perspective (see chapter 9). Even though you are in the midst of excruciatingly difficult circumstances and you may have unbelievable demands on your time, find *at least* twenty minutes each day to focus quietly on God. Even though it may *seem* impossible to steal those moments, the *truth* is, you will lose the battle if you do not stay connected to Christ.

Smoke and Mirrors

Like a dime-store magician, the devil has an arsenal of cheap tricks that will lead you to false conclusions and make things appear other than they are. Guard your heart from falling for this! Pray for discernment, but also enlist some seasoned saints who can give you their perspective.

During chemo my mother's personality changed drastically. She had always been a "handful," but this was far beyond what anyone in my family had ever seen. She became irritable, hostile, and used language that wasn't her norm. Gradually her perceptions became more and more distorted, and she flew into irrational tirades over insignificant events. Even worse, I suddenly became the continuous target of her anger. She lashed out with poisonous words that cut me to the core of my being. Though my original goal had been to show her the love of Jesus, I was tempted to either strike back or run for cover!

During the months that this went on I consoled myself with the knowledge that medications and the strains of illness were speaking. Even so, our poisoned interactions were painful to me and clouded my thinking. I felt I was failing my mother and the Lord.

Fortunately, God brought help in the form of Auntie Vernie, Mom's youngest sister, who saw the situation with different eyes. She agreed that chemo was certainly a factor in my mother's mood swings, but urged me to consider another cause for the tension. The battle being waged over my mother's soul was intensifying, and both of us were being attacked. Because I came representing Christ, my mother pulled away from me at times, just as she was pulling away from Him. She was grappling with a sense of conviction and the feeling that all was not well with her soul. The anger she displayed was not really with me, but part of her own internal struggle. It kept her in the natural realm, where she wouldn't have to think about God. Likewise, as I focused on her scorn and nursed my wounds, I remained in the natural realm, and was rendered powerless. For Satan, this was the ultimate win-win situation.

CALL IN REINFORCEMENTS

It is important not to fight this battle alone. Your goal is to win the war, not to earn a medal of valor for fighting single-handedly. Therefore, when the battle becomes fierce, you may need to call in reinforcements who can divert the enemy and give you the protection you need while you are fighting. Recognizing your need for assistance and acting on that will allow you to stay strong and achieve your objective. However, if you insist on fighting by yourself, you may become weary or wounded, and ultimately sacrifice the mission.

At times it will suffice to draw on the resources of your personal support team comprised of those closest to you. When the battle is more fierce, you will need additional backup and a wider net of protection. This is the time to contact the extended Christian body and ask for prayer. Your pastor and church prayer chain are logical choices (if your church is large and the pastor doesn't know you personally, at least be in contact with someone on the pastoral staff), but this is also a wonderful time to ask friends to have their churches pray for you and your loved one.

If you are typically a more private person and are not accustomed to making your requests known to other people, make an exception this time. Let the prayers of the body of Christ uphold and sustain you. Like it or not, this is how the Holy Spirit has chosen to work in the world, and this battle is no time to miss out on the benefits. God has a special way of calling seasoned warriors into the front lines, so don't be surprised if someone turns up unexpectedly wanting to pray for you. This is the Lord showing you He is working on your behalf.

WEAR YOUR ARMOR

During this intense spiritual fighting, read and reread Ephesians 6:10–18, the passage on spiritual armor. This will remind you to "put on" truth, righteousness, the preparation of the gospel of peace, faith, salvation, and the Word of God, and will help you remember the enemy's tactics. While my parents were dying, I used this passage as a daily prayer and tried to envision all the components I needed for protection and for penetrating enemy territory.

PICK UP YOUR SWORD ·

God has provided only one weapon against the enemy, and that is His Word. Even if you are fully decked out in your armor, without your sword you are defenseless. Knowing this, the enemy will try everything he can to separate you from your weapon. While it is true that illness brings myriad time constraints, there are still ways for you to pick up your sword and keep it sharpened while attending to all the demands of life. It is imperative that you do this.

Staying connected to God's Word during this time does not have to mean hours of study with a commentary and Greek dictionary, even if that is your usual method. Give yourself the grace that is appropriate for the circumstances you are experiencing. Perhaps now you might meditate on a single verse each day, or even one per week. Write the verse on a small card and keep it with you when you are at the hospital or your loved one's home. Or utilize a devotional book with short, meaningful lessons on Scripture (see the appendix for suggestions). The Lord knows the burdens you are carrying and your time constraints and can speak to you in new ways now. Your job is to find time for Him so He can keep your sword sharp and ready to use.

STAND FIRM

Though the enemy will viciously attack you with his full arsenal of evil, and though he is intent on destroying your loved one, he is bound by certain rules of engagement. There are God-ordained limits to what he can do, and even as he fights against you with all his might, he is aware of this. You must meet his bluff. In the meantime, he will relentlessly strive to influence your loved one's free choice and try to discourage you enough so that you will quit fighting. He is hoping you will retreat and seal his victory.

There are times when you won't know how to fight, or may look around you and see the sure signs of defeat. The battle isn't over yet, and God is fighting alongside you, so don't give up! Even if you aren't sure how to move forward, at least stand firm. Wear your armor, keep your sword at the ready, and ignore the taunting of the enemy and the fear he whispers into your heart. Do all that God asks of you, and then wait to see what He will do on your behalf. The miracle you long for may be just around the corner.

Therefore, take up the full armor of God, so that you will be able to resist in the evil day, and having done everything, to stand firm.
—EPHESIANS 6:13

I know what it is to stand firm in the battle for a soul. For me, it meant returning anger with kindness and serving quietly without complaining, fighting back, or begrudging time away from my "real life." It took incredible strength and discipline to stand firm, but these were made possible by faith that the One fighting for me would accomplish His will.

Unexpectedly and without explanation, my mother's anger

was suddenly gone—not just the anger over her illness, but all the bitterness that had plagued her soul for years. During the last months of her life she experienced a complete spiritual transformation, which allowed her relationship with Christ to flourish and brought healing to other relationships, as well. She became more sweet and loving toward me during that time than at any other time I can remember. Though I had worried our last days would be marked by distance, miraculously, we became closer than ever before. The enemy is mighty, but the One who fights for us is mightier still.

Be Still, My Soul

Be still, my soul: the Lord is on thy side;
Bear patiently the cross of grief or pain;
Leave to thy God to order and provide:
In every change He faithful will remain.
Be still, my soul: thy best, thy heavenly Friend
Through thorny ways leads to a joyful end.

Be still my soul: the hour is hastening on
When we shall be forever with the Lord,
When disappointment, grief and fear are gone,
Sorrow forgot, love's purest joys restored.
Be still my soul: when change and tears are past,
All safe and blessed we shall meet at last.
    —Katharina von Schlegel (b. 1697)
        Translated by Jane L. Borthwick (b. 1813)

CHAPTER 11

Endurance

Love never gives up, never loses faith, is always hopeful,
and endures through every circumstance.

—1 CORINTHIANS 13:7 NLT

My friend Vicky took care of her dying mother for several years, so when I found out my mom had cancer, I went to Vicky for advice. She told me about her experience, both negative and positive. I, in turn, described my plans to rearrange work and clear my personal schedule so as to be completely available for my mother. I would travel to another city to care for her until she could move to the house across the street, which my husband was renovating for her (an arrangement that began before she became ill). I listed the responsibilities I would take on and described what I could give up in order to fit them in my life.

Vicky had been down this road before and knew what was required. I had expected her to applaud my willingness to set my own needs aside. Instead, with the wisdom of experience, she gently told me, "It might not be such a good idea to *clear* your schedule. Maybe right now you should keep your life as normal as possible for as long as you can, because a time is coming when you will *have* to make changes. If you give up everything now, you won't have anything left at the end."

Vicky was right. While I thought my wholehearted enthusiasm would save the day, she understood that endurance was what I really needed. Her admonition made me realize this journey would be longer and more rigorous than I anticipated, and I would need to pace myself to get to the finish line. This is true for you, too.

TAKE CARE OF YOURSELF

Walking alongside someone on the homebound journey is not an easy task. It is a marathon race, and only those who plan well will survive the course. Just like an elite athlete, you must take precautions to perform at your peak, prevent injury, and maintain energy. Be deliberate about taking care of yourself, and find time for activities that recharge you. Keep your life as normal as possible for as long as you can, for like Vicky said, one day you will *have* to make changes. In the meantime, take care of yourself so you can offer your best to your loved one at the time it is most needed.

Many of my friends who have cared for dying loved ones have shared with me the things they did to maintain their own physical, emotional, and spiritual well-being. Their ideas are listed below. Use these or create your own to come up with at least one activity you can do on a weekly or bimonthly basis to nurture yourself and keep your batteries charged.

- Exercise regularly
- Eat healthy foods
- Limit intake of sugar, caffeine, and alcohol
- Play a game of golf
- Go fishing
- Take a nap
- Make a standing appointment for a manicure, pedicure, facial, or massage

- Read a good book
- Attend a play
- Sing in the choir
- Go to the museum
- Work on a craft or art project
- Get out of town (see "Respite Care" in chapter 9)
- Go to a movie
- Have lunch with a friend
- Make a play date with your kids or grandkids
- Attend a support group

It may sound silly, but something that really helped build my own endurance was *The Lord of the Rings* movie trilogy. Intended to communicate the Gospel in mythical form, the stories are rich with spiritual meaning, especially for anyone on a journey such as ours. As I watched Frodo suffer, falter, and eventually accomplish his mission of saving Middle Earth, I identified with his struggle and was inspired by his bravery and tenacity. The forces of evil tried to destroy him at every turn and prevent him from completing his mission. Layer upon layer of meaning emerged for me as I watched the Hobbit battle the forces of evil. Something in me rose up and said, *"I can do this! I will keep going!"*

It doesn't matter what sustains you, but it is imperative that you find something to nourish you and keep you moving forward toward the goal. While you tend to the needs of others, be sure to water the garden of your own soul.

Not that I have already attained, or am already perfected; but I press on, that I may lay hold of that for which Christ Jesus has also laid hold of me. Brethren, I do not count myself to have apprehended; but one thing I do, forgetting those things which are behind and reaching forward to those things which are ahead, I press toward the goal for the prize of the upward call of God in Christ Jesus.

—Philippians 3:12–14 NKJV

Set Boundaries

Although it is important to maintain normalcy as long as possible, your commitments will change as you devote more and more time to the needs of your dying loved one. To take care of yourself, it may become necessary to set clear boundaries with other people who do not understand your circumstances and who expect you to continue your usual activities and obligations. While guarding those aspects of your life that are compulsory or that feed you, you may decide to off-load less important duties during this time. People affected by your decisions may object, but by enforcing your boundaries you will protect yourself from burnout. Prioritize carefully, and prune away unnecessary or unfruitful areas. Though the process may be painful, it is only temporary and will allow you to devote yourself to your loved one without losing your sanity or your health.

Even more difficult than setting boundaries with your friends and colleagues is the process of setting boundaries with your family. The dynamics of the family are greatly intensified during the time when someone is ill, and any dysfunction that was previously present becomes exaggerated. This is not only an unfortunate waste of time and energy but is also a tremendous distraction from the spiritual matters on which you need to focus your attention. Be mindful that some family members will purposely bring their own agenda with them and will try to manipulate everyone else in order to accomplish their goals. Others who are needy or damaged will simply require attention and will not be able to help care for the dying person. Worst of all is the toxic family member whose very presence poisons the atmosphere. The spiritual debris that comes with this type of person stirs up agitation and interferes with what you are trying to do for your loved one. No matter what your family is like, by setting some clear boundaries you can effectively deal with even the most challenging individuals.

If your loved one lives independently or is in the hospital, try to schedule your visits for times when drama-loving family members are not likely to be present. Or, if this is not possible, take another believer with you who can serve as a buffer and as prayer support. Like a sentry on duty, your friend can silently pray for you and your loved one and thereby be a tremendous help. Another benefit to taking someone else with you is that family members are less likely to behave inappropriately when an outsider is present.

If your loved one lives with you, it is imperative that you set boundaries for the acceptable times and parameters of visits and other behaviors in your home. It is very disruptive to care for a dying person, and most people (even well meaning ones) do not realize the tremendous burden you are carrying. It is not necessary for you to receive visitors at all times of the day or night, or to accommodate what is most convenient for others. Ask them to adjust their schedule to something that is reasonable for you. Do not hesitate to set visiting hours that are suitable for you and decline requests outside of those times. Toward the end this may need to change, but if you will be caring for your loved one over a long period of time, your family and friends must respect your need to maintain normalcy in your home as much as possible.

Because caregivers are already doing so much, family members can easily take advantage of them and add to their already heavy workload, even without meaning to do so. Therefore, it may be necessary to educate your loved ones about other ways they can assist you. For instance, something as small as the use of disposable plates, cups, and utensils for meals and snacks will greatly alleviate extra tasks for you. If your family is not of the mindset to clean up after themselves, be sure to provide these items and lovingly but firmly request their use. Also decide in advance whether you are willing to have out-of-town family members stay in your home when they come either to visit your loved one or later for the funeral. If having guests is not comfortable for you, ask friends whether they would be willing to entertain on your behalf, or provide information about local accommodations well in advance. Boundaries such as these are often difficult to initially put into place, but doing so will protect you so that you can actually continue to serve your loved one in a more meaningful way.

The most difficult boundaries to set are between you and your dying loved one. When a person is ill, it is natural for that person to become more self-focused than at other times. It would be wonderful if all terminally ill patients could have a sweet disposition, be thoughtful and considerate at all times, and never want to trouble anyone else. However, this isn't reality. And even individuals who normally possess all these characteristics are often unable to maintain them during illness. As the body deteriorates, your loved one will need more and more assistance from you (and perhaps from others, as well). Constant adjustments will be necessary, often prompting you to rise to new levels of selflessness. Even so, it is healthy and appropriate for you to set reasonable boundaries with your loved one so that issues that might otherwise seem insignificant and completely tolerable will not discourage you, block communication, or thwart your efforts to provide spiritual care.

My friend Linda and her husband invested a great amount of effort and expense to create beautiful and self-contained "mother-in-law quarters" in their home for Linda's frail and elderly parents. As her father's health declined, Linda also served as his caregiver. From the time her parents came to stay, Linda adjusted her meal planning to take into consideration their habits and tastes, often at the expense of her children's preferences. Instead of being appreciative, Linda's mother responded by continually criticizing the meals during dinner conversation and complaining about what was being served. Though Linda is normally very resilient, her mother's cutting remarks became extremely depressing to her. Finally she had a meeting with her mother and set a boundary. Linda said she would be willing to cook one family meal each week, but each woman would prepare dinner separately for all the other evening meals. In this way, the two family units were able to maintain their own preferences, and Linda and her mother were able to avoid unnecessary discord.

After my eighty-four-year-old father was widowed, his health deteriorated very rapidly. Clearly he was going to need assistance on a daily basis. Determined that Dad wouldn't be relegated to the care of strangers, my brother and sister-in-law brought him into their home to live. Immediately afterward he suffered a series of strokes that left him completely immobilized and unable to care for himself. Admirably, Stan and Kristy were unwavering in their decision and made the necessary adjustments to provide for our seriously debilitated father. Kristy even quit her job so that she could provide around-the-clock care. Dad was genuinely appreciative of their efforts, and at first was reluctant to impose upon them. But as time went by, he became increasingly demanding and less thoughtful of their needs. He would sometimes sulk and complain if he wasn't the center of attention. He often treated Kristy disrespectfully, and ordered her about as though she were an employee (or servant!) who was failing miserably in her duties. At the time, their daughter was a senior in high school, and Dad seemed to resent time spent with her, almost as though they were competitors.

Stan and Kristy understood that Dad was suffering greatly and recognized the fact that his inability to be self-sufficient caused him to be irritable. Still they knew they had to set boundaries with him in order to maintain a positive atmosphere in their home and to make a stressful situation tolerable over the long haul. After reassuring Dad that they loved him and would always provide for his care, they clearly defined behaviors they considered to be unacceptable and inappropriate. They also came to workable compromises that would allow him what he needed but still keep their family routine somewhat intact. Open communication about these matters allowed everyone to come to a workable agreement and helped sustain positive relationships in spite of the strains of terminal illness.

Setting boundaries can be very difficult but it can also be very healing. If you need more information on how to set boundaries, see the appendix for resources.

No Need for Martyrs

If you are a caregiver, or if you are spending countless hours in a hospital or convalescent home, you may be stretched further than you ever thought possible. Your choice to help your loved one and to reach out with the love of Christ is admirable, but if you don't keep things in your life that feed you and prune out things that drain you, you will become overloaded, imbalanced, and may start to feel resentful. If you sense you are feeling like a martyr, remember, this is a *choice*. You can walk away at any time. If you choose to stay, ask Jesus to help you have His attitude in service. It is only when we lay down our lives willingly that God can use us to accomplish His eternal purpose.

LOOK TO JESUS

Jesus is the perfect model of endurance. During His ministry, He was pulled in a thousand different directions, constantly gave to others, and experienced rejection and suffering in return. Yet He knew His goal and kept a single focus to accomplish it. Though He made himself available to others, He also knew how to set boundaries and found times for private spiritual renewal. Who can better understand your situation? When you are tired, weary, and don't know if you can keep going, look to Him.

> Let us run with endurance the race that is set before us,
> looking unto Jesus, the author and finisher of our faith,
> who for the joy that was set before Him endured the cross,
> despising the shame, and has sat down at the right hand of
> the throne of God. For consider Him who has endured
> such hostility from sinners against Himself, lest you
> become weary and discouraged.
> —HEBREWS 12:1–3 NKJV

> If you follow this advice, and if God directs you to do so,
> then you will be able to endure the pressures, and all these
> people will go home in peace.
> —EXODUS 18:23 NLT

CHAPTER 12

God's Covenant Love

*Therefore know that the Lord your God, He is God, the
faithful God who keeps covenant and mercy for a
thousand generations with those who love Him
and keep His commandments.*

—DEUTERONOMY 7:9 NKJV

In times of crisis, God often reaches out to us in more tangible ways than at other times. I believe this is a special mercy He bestows on us to get us through circumstances that would otherwise be unbearable. He might choose to send a person to us who says exactly what we need to hear, or provide some gift of beauty, like a sunset or a rainbow that flashes His banner of love across the sky. Or He may provide a message from His Word that seems to be written precisely for this moment in time. That is what He did for me while my stepmother, Rita, was dying.

I was still grieving the recent death of my mother when I decided to join a *Precept Upon Precept** Bible study group. *Precept*

*Precept Upon Precept studies by Kay Arthur are published by Precept Ministries International of Chattanooga, TN.

classes are extremely challenging and rival any class I took in Bible college. The mental stimulation, the love and support of the class members, and the truths I was learning in God's Word all became part of the healing process for my war-weary soul.

Then came the phone call that brought all the suffocating experiences of death crashing down on me again. My step-mother, Rita, had been struggling with cancer, and word came that it had spread to her liver. Nothing could be done. The doctor expected her to survive only a few weeks and had sent her home to die.

I experienced all the normal reactions to this kind of news—disbelief, numbness, and fear. I flashed back to my mother's illness and death, only ten months earlier, and felt all the heaviness and fatigue returning. It seemed far too soon to face these same challenges one more time. From the depths of my broken heart, I cried out to God: "Please, Lord, it's too soon! I can't do this *again!*" At the same moment those words came out of my mouth, I was overcome with a sense of peace and assurance. I knew I was meant to walk Rita home to Jesus. This was a task set before me to do, and I knew the Lord would provide what was needed.

If there was anything I learned while my mother was dying, it is that people want answers in times of crisis. Death is the worst crisis of all, and facing it can lead to spiritual openness. My mother's heart changed drastically during her illness, and had finally become pliable in God's hands. Before her death, she yielded her heart fully to Christ. The journey had indeed been brutal, but the rewards had been well worth it. I sensed it would be the same with Rita. She had already opened up to me over the last several months about her beliefs, fears, and questions about God. Now that her situation was dire, she would probably want to resolve these issues. Rita had asked me to come to her. My husband and I both agreed I should go.

My dad and Rita lived about fifty miles away. I was teaching part-time in the music department of a Christian university in their county, and since I could easily make the commute from their home, I moved in with them, ready to stay as long as necessary. Three of us—Rita's daughter, a close friend, and I—set up a rotation system, making sure at least one of us was always there. Besides work, my only stipulation for being part of the team was that I be able to go home on Friday mornings for my Bible study group. At the time, we were studying all the covenants in the Bible, and I had found the information to be extremely rich and life-changing. The study emphasized the continuity of the Old and New Testaments and showed how salvation was foreshadowed even in the Lord's relationship with Abraham and the Israelites. I had no idea how important that study would be during the journey ahead.

My favorite times with Rita were our late-night visits, when the rest of the house was asleep. In the last stages of a person's life, the internal clock disappears, resulting in strange sleeping patterns. Rita often woke up at three o'clock in the morning, wide awake and ready to talk. I volunteered to take the night shift with her and looked forward to our intimate early-morning chats. These conversations often drifted into spiritual territory and almost always ended in prayer. Rita was hungry for closeness with God but confided she saw Him as a tyrant who was concerned with rules and regulations. She was also angry with Him for things that had happened in the past. Fortunately, my Bible study provided me with Scriptures at my fingertips that described the kindness, grace, and mercy of the Lord. The things I was learning in my class were not only sustaining *me* spiritually but were also providing answers to Rita's urgent spiritual questions.

GOD'S COVENANT OFFERS HOPE

Rita's condition worsened steadily, and her time on earth was growing short. Her cancerous liver was no longer able to filter poisons from her system, and just as the doctor had predicted, the toxins began affecting her brain. She was still lucid most of the time, but sometimes hallucinated or became delirious. We knew she would eventually lapse into a coma and no longer be able to communicate with us. It was a rush against time.

I was somewhat confused about Rita's spiritual condition. I wanted to see a definitive decision for Christ before she died. She had finally admitted to me she believed Jesus was the Son of God and had died for our sins and risen again. She agreed He was the only way to heaven. But still she harbored resentment toward Him. I wasn't *sure* where she was spiritually and knew that soon it would be too late to know.

One night, during our visit, she began to describe a place she was seeing in her mind's eye. I knew those who are nearing death commonly relate experiences of seeing the celestial realm or loved ones who have already passed away, so I was not in the least bit alarmed. In fact, I was insatiably curious, so I kept asking her questions about her experience. She described a beautifully serene place with a river, a waterfall, and lush trees everywhere. There were beings who offered comfort, and she seemed peaceful and at ease as she described the scene. I thought she must surely be seeing a glimpse of heaven and was comforted by this. Suddenly she made a quick movement of her head and scowled in displeasure. Then she looked at me and said, "Hey, are there cell phones in this place?" Though I couldn't help but laugh, her question made me wonder whether she was having a spiritual encounter or just hallucinating.

Rita clung to life tenaciously long after anyone had expected. After a month, she was clearly drifting in and out of consciousness and would sometimes be completely still for days. At the six-week mark, she was hardly with us any longer. I didn't know if she had fully resolved her spiritual issues, but something I had learned about covenants kept my hope alive.

WITH YOU AND YOUR HOUSE

The covenants in the Bible are binding agreements, like contracts. Some are made man-to-man, and others between God and man. All covenant agreements share common elements, and these have great spiritual significance. The covenants are powerful representations of God's nature, and a great deal of theology is based on them. The words *covenant* and *testament* are interchangeable, and the Old Testament contains the covenant of the Law, which required adherence to strict regulations and the use of animal sacrifices to atone for sins. For Christians, the most important of all the covenants is the new covenant, which is salvation through grace. When Jesus instituted communion with His disciples at the Last Supper, He said,

> This cup which is poured out for you is the new covenant in My blood.
> —LUKE 22:20

Paul wrote extensively about the new covenant in several of his letters, often quoting Old Testament prophets who foretold of the new covenant. In the following passage he quotes both Isaiah and Jeremiah:

> The Deliverer will come from Zion,
> He will remove ungodliness from Jacob.
> This is My covenant with them,
> When I take away their sins.
> —ROMANS 11:26–27

As I studied biblical covenants, I became engrossed with the covenants in the Old Testament. I learned that these are a foreshadowing, or "type" of Christ, and have deep symbolism about salvation. Repeatedly a common feature stood out to me. The covenants are never made merely between two individuals but rather the *participants*, their *households*, and their *descendants forever* are all included in the covenant agreement. Throughout the Bible, God continually keeps His covenants and promises, even to those who are unfaithful to Him. In fact, many believe the nation of Israel exists today only because the Lord made a covenant with Abraham (which he later repeated to Jacob, aka *Israel*), promising that the land would belong to his descendants forever (Genesis 17; 28:13–15).

The following are some examples from Scripture (with emphasis added) showing that biblical covenants are inclusive of family members *and* their heirs:

Noah

Then God spoke to Noah and to his sons with him, saying, "Now behold, I Myself do establish My covenant with you, and with your *descendants after you*."
—GENESIS 9:8–9

Abraham

I will establish My covenant between Me and you and your descendants after you throughout their generations for an *everlasting* covenant.
—GENESIS 17:7

David and Jonathan

"You shall not cut off your lovingkindness from my house forever, not even when the Lord cuts off every one of the enemies of David from the face of the earth." So Jonathan made a covenant with the *house of David*, saying, "May the Lord require it at the hands of David's enemies."
—1 SAMUEL 20:15–16

As for the agreement of which you and I have spoken, behold, the Lord is between you and me *forever*.
—1 SAMUEL 20:23

Go in safety, inasmuch as we have sworn to each other in the name of the Lord, saying, "The Lord will be between me and you, and between *my descendants and your descendants forever*."
—1 SAMUEL 20:42

Biblical covenants, which represent God's heart toward us, include extended family and all forthcoming generations. Surely this cannot be translated into a doctrine of guaranteed salvation for our family members, because every individual is responsible for making his or her own choice to receive or reject the gifts of grace and eternal life. However, this characteristic of covenants is repeated throughout the Bible, and therefore its significance cannot be ignored.

One of the most touching examples of this is in the covenant between David and Jonathan. Jonathan, the son of King Saul, risked his own position, the wrath of his father, and possibly even his life in order to help his beloved friend David escape from Saul. Jonathan and Saul were killed in battle, and David was crowned king. Years later David was still bound to his covenant.

> Is there yet anyone left of the house of Saul, that I may
> show him kindness for Jonathan's sake?
> —2 SAMUEL 9:1

David searched his realm for any living heir of Saul or Jonathan and discovered Mephibosheth, Jonathan's son. When his father was slain, five-year-old Mephibosheth's governess whisked him out of the palace, fearing for his life. In the scramble to safety, Mephibosheth fell and was permanently crippled in both feet. David found him living in hiding. Due to his injury, he may have even been living in abject poverty.

When Mephibosheth, Saul's heir, was summoned to David's palace, he likely anticipated a death sentence. Instead, David, in radical generosity, restored to Mephibosheth everything that had belonged to Saul and Jonathan. Imagine! Lands, servants, chariots, livestock, jewels—all these were lavished upon him. Furthermore, he was invited to the royal table and treated as one of David's own sons (2 Samuel 9:1–13).

As I read this beautiful story, I understood that David's gesture is a picture of God's mercy toward us. David extended kindness toward Mephibosheth for only one reason: *he was of the household of Jonathan, with whom David had made a covenant.* David actively searched for him, made a place for him, and included him in his royal family. He bestowed undeserved treasures on Mephibosheth, and then adopted him as his own son. If David, an imperfect man, would do this for Jonathan's relative, what would our perfect God, because of His covenant of salvation with me, be willing to do for one of *my* relatives?

My study of covenants and my experience with dying unbelievers have led me to believe that our heavenly Father extends *every* opportunity to our loved ones because of the grace that was extended to us when we became partakers of the new covenant of His blood. Of course, there is still the element of free will. Mephibosheth could have rejected David's offer, and likewise, our loved ones can reject salvation. But I am convinced that the Lord is even more gracious with our family members than David was with Mephibosheth, and He will lavish His love upon them even to the last possible moment.

A RAINBOW FOR A SIGN

As Thanksgiving approached, Rita's condition was extremely grave. She was no longer responsive, now in her second full week of unconsciousness. I was still part of the caregiving team, and we were just trying to keep her comfortable. I knew others could take care of her physical needs, and I was feeling as though I had done everything I could for her spiritually. I had been with Rita for six weeks, and though I had hoped to be with her until the end, I now had something else on my mind. The one-year anniversary of my mother's death was approaching, and I wanted some space alone to commemorate the day and to honor her apart from Rita. Two days before Thanksgiving I prepared to go home.

Before leaving, I ventured into Rita's bedroom to see her one last time. She was very near death now. Her face was tense, but I didn't know whether it was from physical pain or some inner battle she was fighting. I wanted to do something for her, so I rubbed lotion on her hands and feet, then gently massaged her neck and shoulders. Her face relaxed a bit, and she appeared more at ease. Was she aware of my presence?

I knew I would probably never see her alive again, and wasn't certain whether I would see her again in heaven either. She had made tremendous spiritual strides during our late-night chats, but I still wasn't *sure* if she was saved. Even though I couldn't communicate with her, I felt I could at least pray over her. Perhaps something would connect with her spirit, even in her present state. I began praying aloud, and prayed about everything I could think of, especially those unresolved issues with God. I wanted to leave her bathed in the presence of the Holy Spirit, and invited Him to join us.

I interspersed my prayer with things I wanted to say to Rita. I talked about heaven, describing what I knew of it from Scripture. I explained that there she could have a new body. I spoke of Jesus, reiterating that He is the only way to the Father. Just in case she wasn't clear on the important matters, I laid out the entire plan of salvation, telling her how she could experience it if she wanted to. All she needed was to confess her sins and accept God's gift of eternal life through Jesus Christ. I told her I knew she could no longer speak but that it didn't matter. If she could agree in her spirit and cry out to Jesus in her heart that would be enough.

At that very moment, as if on cue, she let out a long, deliberate moan. I hadn't expected this, and frankly was startled. As I looked at her face now, I saw an expression of concentration. She was trying with all her might to communicate with me. Years earlier, when I had myself been a patient near death, I experienced a twilight state in which I could fully hear and understand voices, but was powerless to respond to them. This seemed to be happening with Rita. So when I spoke again, I did so as though she could fully understand me.

My heart raced with excitement as I carried on my "conversation" with her. I began to sense a strong presence of the Holy Spirit in the room. For six weeks I had been hoping for something dramatic to take place, and strange as it was, this time of prayer seemed to be the culmination of all our visits. Her face finally had an expression of peace, and it appeared that some unseen transaction had taken place. Knowing my job was finished, I leaned over and kissed Rita's forehead one last time. I drove to the university to teach my voice students, and later that night finally slept in my own bed.

The next morning I phoned my dad to see how Rita was doing. He was weeping, and told me Rita had slipped away just a few moments before I called. The news of her death hit me like a bullet to the chest. Even though I had fully expected it, I was crushed and suddenly filled with doubt. Had she ever come to a place of faith? I had the overwhelming sense I had failed her and failed in my mission. Falling to my knees, I sobbed out to God, "O Lord, let me know whether she knew you. Please show me a sign!"

As soon as the words left my mouth, I regretted saying them. After all, Jesus rebuked those who wanted a sign, and I knew I had no right to ask this. Repentant, I prayed until my composure returned. I washed my face, and then forced myself to go through the motions of unpacking and trying to settle back into my life.

Though I am not usually aware of it, my husband tells me I have a habit of constantly singing, no matter what I am doing. Often a tune sticks with me for days, and I sing or hum the same phrase over and over until I wear it out. The previous day, I worked with one of my soprano students on an aria from Handel's *Messiah*, and now I couldn't get that song out of my head. I usually love the text to *Rejoice Greatly, O Daughter of Zion*, but on this day those words couldn't have been further from my mood.

Suddenly I listened to what I was singing. What a strange juxtaposition to be on my face grieving Rita's death one moment and then singing *Rejoice!* the very next. Of all the songs that could have stuck in my memory, why that one?

Every bit of Handel's *Messiah* is taken straight from Scripture. My *Precept* classes have trained me to always look at the context of biblical passages, so I decided this must apply to scriptural song texts as well. I stopped what I was doing, got out my

Strong's Concordance, and did some research. What I found astounded me!

> Rejoice greatly, O daughter of Zion!
> Shout in triumph, O daughter of Jerusalem!
> Behold, your king is coming to you;
> He is just and endowed with salvation,
> Humble and mounted on a donkey. . . .
>
> As for you also, because of the blood of *My covenant* with you, I have set your prisoners free from the waterless pit.
>
> —ZECHARIAH 9:9, 11 (emphasis added)

Before I finished reading the passage, I was weeping. How could the message be more clear? In my weeks of studying biblical covenants, I had seen God's love dramatically displayed in them. I had suspected He was extending His covenant love to my family. Now He had placed a rainbow in the heavens as a sign for me, just as He had done with Noah! Through a song more than two hundred fifty years old, the Holy Spirit led me to a verse that served as confirmation of God's faithfulness and of Rita's faith. Because of His covenant with me, He had set my stepmother free!

The Lord is so good and so amazing! He used a piece of classical music—my native musical language—combined with a key concept from my Bible study class to reassure me that my loved one had found her way to Jesus. He set a captive free and had graciously let me *know* what had taken place.

These words were not only meant for me. They are also for you. God loves His people and has a covenant relationship with us. He wants those covenants to extend to the people in our lives whom we love, including the person you are carrying on your heart today. He is not willing for any to perish, and He will provide every possible opportunity for salvation. He wants to set your prisoner free, too. Trust Him!

CHAPTER 13

Making Arrangements

My evil genius Procrastination has whispered to me
to tarry till a more convenient season.
—MARY TODD LINCOLN

My friend Bev phoned me early one morning to tell me her father had died suddenly. She was heading to Florida to be with her family and would call again when she could. The next time we spoke the funeral had already taken place, and I asked how it had gone. "It was amazing," Bev said. "Daddy had taken care of *everything*, so all *we* had to do was grieve."

Curtis had been in the life insurance business and was well acquainted with the confusion and panic that families experience when death occurs unexpectedly. Wanting to spare his loved ones this trauma, he had made every necessary arrangement in advance. He also created a well-organized file with very specific instructions and proof of payment for the funeral and related expenses. His life insurance information and necessary documents were all in order. Every detail had been executed, down to the music for his service. His careful planning was the last and most thoughtful gift he gave his family. Most of us will not be this fortunate. Even when a terminal illness exists, the subjects of death and funerals are often taboo, and conversations about them are avoided like the proverbial elephant in the living room. Family members are then left to scramble to prepare a service and are sometimes at a loss for how to proceed.

Even if your loved one is not willing to discuss his or her wishes, *you* can begin thinking ahead about what will need to be done at the time of death. This will take some of the shock value away and will empower you to act more decisively when the time comes. And if you are comfortable talking about these issues, you may be able to help other family members who find this topic more difficult.

It is sometimes easier for a person to discuss his or her wishes about final arrangements with someone outside of the family. With fewer emotional ties, discussions can be more objective and matter-of-fact. Although this may cause some family members to become upset or feel excluded, it is important to provide adequate emotional space in which your loved one can grapple with these very personal decisions. Be understanding of the fact that this issue is emotionally charged, and professionals such as funeral directors or social workers can often facilitate more objective and effective conversations about it. Be sensitive to the needs of your loved one, and also to others concerned. If appropriate, promote nonthreatening conversations that will help clarify any arrangements yet to be made.

As with so many aspects of the dying process, your loved one is watching your reactions and scrutinizing your behavior. How you deal with this topic is one more opportunity for gaining credibility with your unbelieving loved one. Even if you or other family members feel as though you are left hanging without knowing how to attend to funeral details that will eventually be needed, don't be caught unnecessarily pushing your loved one into making decisions. Though it is much easier to deal with these matters in advance, thousands of people die every day without prior notice, and their families manage to put services together for them. As much as possible, let your loved one remain in charge, even if that means avoiding an uncomfortable topic. Being perceived as an advocate and facilitator is preferable to accomplishing a task while trampling on the feelings of someone you love.

Depending on the personalities of those involved, and also upon the current state of affairs, discussions of this nature can be extremely exhausting or lead to huge emotional responses. This is partly because the idea of death suddenly becomes very real and undeniable. If you decide to initiate a conversation on this topic, be sure to choose the time and atmosphere carefully and with a great deal of prayer. The Holy Spirit can transform this otherwise uncomfortable discussion into something He can use to draw your loved one another step closer toward Home.

A creative way to broach this subject is to access the many sources on the Internet for funeral planning. The one I like best is *www.funeralplan.com,* which includes a free guide that can be printed or filled out online. This resource or one like it will help your loved one and family members understand the various choices that are possible and determine which ones are most suitable.

A side benefit of preplanning is that it reduces the chances of painful disputes that can arise later. Any tensions already existing among family members are amplified after a loved one dies. When no arrangements have been made or wishes relayed, the family is left open to the possibility of a free-for-all that will ultimately leave someone feeling angry or wounded. In contrast, when preferences are clearly stated or better yet, put in writing, it is much easier for everyone to work together toward the common goal of carrying out those plans.

THINGS TO CONSIDER

After someone dies a very strange thing happens. Your loved one suddenly becomes known as "the body" or "the remains."

No longer will the person be referred to as "your mother," "Mr. Smith," or "the patient." This change in terminology can be very abrupt, sometimes not giving you time to absorb the weight of the loss. Be prepared for this inevitable change, or you will be shocked by the severity of it.

Generally the next of kin has legal authority for disposition of remains. However, specific written clarification will prevent unnecessary complications or delays. This matter is best addressed as part of the advance directive, and should be part of your emergency file or notebook.

CHOOSING A FUNERAL HOME

Even if nothing else is done before the time of death, make a firm decision about which funeral home will be used. At the time of death, it will be necessary to specify where your loved one will be taken, and if you are not familiar with local facilities, you may find yourself fumbling to think of one. Generally it is best to use a funeral home that is geographically convenient. If your loved one lives in one city and most of the people who will attend the service live somewhere else, it is always possible to have the body transported to a facility in another city for the funeral.

Often significant savings can be obtained by purchasing pre-need packages. The savings are likely to apply only if the purchase is several months in advance of death, not just a few weeks. Making the arrangements prior to need also guarantees the cost, even if the funeral home raises its prices later. Some people are hesitant to pay for funeral services in advance, and wonder what would happen if the funeral home should go out of business. However, funeral homes are required to follow strict guidelines regarding this issue. They are not allowed to actually receive money for services that are not yet rendered. Therefore, any payment that is made is held in trust on behalf of your loved one. If the funeral home should go out of business, the fees are transferred to another facility.

Funerals vary greatly in price and are generally more costly than cremation. However, if your loved one chooses to be cremated, keep in mind that not all funeral homes offer this service. Be sure to determine the closest facility that can handle this request.

In some cities, caskets can be obtained at lower costs through casket retailers. If you decide to utilize this option, check with the funeral home before making a purchase. Although they are required by law to accept a casket that has been purchased elsewhere, they generally will accept delivery of the coffin only on the day of the funeral. Without prior planning, this could cause a serious inconvenience!

AT THE TIME OF DEATH

If your loved one dies in the hospital or other care facility, a doctor will be summoned to pronounce death. Afterward, a hospital staff member will ask where the body should be taken, at which time you will indicate the funeral home that has been chosen (sometimes this designation is made earlier with the hospital social worker). It is advisable to keep the name, address, and phone number tucked inside a wallet or purse for quick and easy reference in case you are unable to think clearly at the time this information is requested.

If the person dies at home, there are two possible scenarios. First, be sure to take note of the time your loved one passes away. This information will be needed for the death certificate.

If your loved one has been under hospice care, the hospice staff will give you instructions in advance for exactly what to do. In most cases, the hospice agency must be contacted. Frequently, the nurse then comes to the home to pronounce death and will call the funeral home on behalf of the family. However, *it is not necessary to call hospice immediately.* If you or other family members need some time with your loved one, or if you are waiting for someone else to arrive, it is perfectly acceptable to wait before calling the nurse. Just remember that once the call is placed, events will happen in fairly rapid succession.

The funeral director will arrive at the home with an ambulance for transporting the body. At this time, it is wise to sequester yourself somewhere away from your loved one, and let the hospice nurse handle this for you. Remember, your loved one has now become "the body." Though nothing disrespectful will be done, seeing your lifeless loved one wrapped in a sheet and rolled on a gurney may be very upsetting to you. If your hospice does not provide this service, designate an appropriate friend to do it, and call that person at the time of death.

If your loved one is not on hospice care, the death *must* be reported to local authorities. Call 9-1-1 immediately after your loved one dies. Paramedics will arrive and pronounce death. Afterward, police will be summoned for a brief investigation and will communicate with the coroner's office. Once all these matters have been attended to, the funeral director will come to the home to transport the body (this potential drama is one excellent reason for choosing hospice care).

DEATH CERTIFICATES

Death certificates are needed in order to take care of any financial or legal transactions such as finalizing burial or cremation, closing bank accounts, collecting life insurance, transferring funds to beneficiaries, and transferring property titles. The funeral director will ask you the number of certificates you would like him to order. The more complicated your loved one's estate, the more certificates will be needed, so it is helpful to estimate in advance the approximate number of certificates you will need. When my mother died, I requested fifteen certificates and found this to be more than adequate.

To order the death certificates, you will need to know your loved one's full legal name, date and place of birth, and Social Security number. Additionally, you must provide military rank and serial number (if applicable), and the names and birthplaces of your loved one's parents. If you are not already familiar with this information, it is best to obtain it from your loved one before he or she is unable to share it.

Other details to discuss are:

1. Burial or cremation?
2. Cemetery, mausoleum, niche, urn, or ashes scattered?
3. Funeral or memorial service? Graveside service?
4. Religious or non-religious?
5. Military honors? Flag presentation and/or gun salute?
6. Who will officiate?
7. Church, funeral home, or other location?
8. If casket, wood or metal? Frugal or lavish? Purchase in advance?
9. Memorial cards?
10. Printed order of service or program?
11. Eulogy? Who will deliver? Content?
12. Music?
13. Flowers?
14. Grave marker or headstone? What inscription?
15. Will there be an obituary published? Who will write it? What is to be included?
16. Will any photos be used for the service? Will any be taken?
17. Does date need to take into consideration out-of-town travelers?
18. Where will out-of-towners stay?
19. Will there be a gathering afterward? Where? Will there be food?
20. Who is responsible for payment or financial arrangements?

PART FOUR

Journey's End

CHAPTER 14

The Invisible Work

Live on the east side of the mountain. It's the sunrise side.
It is the side to see the day that is coming, not to see
the day that has gone.

—TOM LEA

The losses that accompany illness and death are painfully obvious. We watch them in the gaunt face and diminishing stature of our loved one, and turn them over in our minds as we contemplate a future with a huge, gaping hole in it. Yes, we are sadly aware of the losses. The gains, however, are just as real, but they often arrive through work that is invisible.

The apostle Paul talked about these gains:

We live in the face of death. . . . Though our bodies are dying, our spirits are being renewed every day. For our present troubles are quite small and won't last very long. Yet they produce for us an immeasurably great glory that will last forever! So we don't look at the troubles we can

see right now; rather, we look forward to what we have
not yet seen. For the troubles we see will soon be over, but
the joys to come will last forever.

—2 Corinthians 4:12, 16–18 nlt

Paul knew that when a body begins to waste away, a remarkable renewal happens in the spiritual realm. This paradox goes against our way of thinking, but is true nevertheless. So even though your loved one may seem to be losing ground physically, don't underestimate the spiritual work that is taking place. On the outside, what is happening may appear tragic, but in truth, it may be the answer to your prayers.

There is a thin veil separating this world from the spiritual realm. As the dying process begins, that veil becomes increasingly transparent, allowing the person to see glimpses of the spiritual realm. This is a time when the person may become fully aware of the reality of eternity and the need for reconciliation with God. Kay Arthur was a nurse before she became a Bible teacher, and tells the story of a patient who went into cardiac arrest while she was on duty. She and a doctor worked frantically to save the man, who kept slipping away and then reviving. Each time his heart began beating again, he would scream out in desperation and plead for the doctor to keep him alive, for he said he had just seen the flames of hell. This is a vivid reminder of how real the spiritual realm is to those who are dying.

Usually, awareness of eternity arrives in less dramatic ways and is imperceptible to observers. In fact, the only apparent change may be increased stillness. The person may begin to sleep for extremely long periods, often twenty or more hours each day, or go in and out of consciousness. These changes can initially be alarming, but it is important to remember that the Holy Spirit is able to move in your loved one's mind and spirit even during extended times of sleep, unconsciousness, or coma. It is as though the person now has one foot in the physical world and one in the spiritual realm. Poised between the two in this way, your loved one may be more closely attuned to the voice of God than you could imagine. Therefore, avoid the temptation to rouse the person, for by doing so, you might interrupt the invisible work of the Holy Spirit.

Many stories have been relayed to me by those who have been near the dying and have understood that a supernatural exchange has occurred during what appeared outwardly to be nothing more than deep slumber. Evidence of this spiritual work may come in the form of new understanding or resolve that seems to be suddenly present. Your loved one may awaken with an urgent determination to repair relationships, communicate last wishes, or make known spiritually transforming revelations. Things you have unsuccessfully tried to explain may now suddenly become crystal clear, or you may observe a new level of peace or inner strength you have not previously seen. Remember, your loved one is now on an accelerated spiritual track in preparation for death. Because you are more grounded here in the physical world, this may be difficult for you to understand.

During this time of spiritual transition, you can still make a great contribution by bathing the person in prayer. If sleep is extremely deep, it may even be possible to enter the room and pray aloud without causing any disturbance. You may also want to sing, or even provide recorded hymns, praise music, or Scripture that will help usher in the presence of the Lord. All these things will help provide a positive atmosphere. Other than that and keeping your loved one physically comfortable, there is little else you can do now. This is the time when the Holy Spirit will speak directly to your loved one. It is your time to wait.

CHAPTER 15

Giving Gifts

*Thou who wouldst give, give quickly. In the grave thy
loved ones can receive no kindness.*
—THOMAS CARLYLE

Much of the dying process is about fighting for survival. However, there comes a time when the fighting ceases, and is replaced with peace and surrender. This is a significant shift, and while it may make your loved one more comfortable, it may be difficult for you. It is one thing to walk alongside someone on a difficult journey, but a completely different thing to realize the journey is now coming to an end, and you will soon part company.

One way to make this process a bit easier is to give gifts to one another. These are not worldly treasures, for those mean little in light of what is taking place. Rather, these are gifts that define what people mean to one another and promise "you will never be forgotten." These are legacies that prove our lives have been changed because we have walked side by side, and that will be cherished once we go our separate ways. These are the things that will remain when everything else is gone.

Your loved one may have gifts to give to you and others. Whether or not this is the case, you can give gifts—to your loved one and to those who will mourn. You can initiate the process, because you understand the importance of it. You can make the difference.

MENDING FENCES

One of the most important gifts that can be given during this time is forgiveness. The person who is dying may be the one to seek forgiveness or may be the one who must grant it to another. Either way, it can be a painful process. Sometimes the things that have been done need to be named and said aloud. In other cases, it may be enough to let the person know he or she is loved in spite of wrongs that were committed. Whether you must settle unfinished business with your loved one or whether you serve as the facilitator for others, God will show you how far to go and will put the right words on your heart.

If you are not directly involved but are aware of an incident that is causing your loved one or someone else deep pain, commit yourself to pray for that situation. Ask God to let it be resolved before your loved one dies. If it seems right, you might initiate a visit that could lead to healing. If it isn't your dispute, don't feel compelled to try to solve it or interfere, but you can provide a listening ear and even serve as a sounding board or intermediary, if appropriate.

If your loved one makes a specific request to see someone, take heed. If there is unfinished business, your loved one may "hold on" until accounts can be settled. If for some reason a face-to-face meeting is impossible, a phone call or letter may satisfy. Offer to assist with these efforts.

The need to impart or receive forgiveness before death can become vastly significant. Remember, the Lord is wooing your loved one, and repentance and forgiveness are essential components to that process. If this issue becomes a primary focus, be prepared to reassure your loved one with Scriptures that reflect

God's promise of forgiveness (see the appendix).

One of the most profound examples of the need to resolve old issues was relayed to me by a hospice nurse. One of her patients, an elderly woman, had been expected to die for several months. Her tenacity and ability to cling to life had mystified everyone, including her nurse, who had no explanation. One day, while the nurse was present, the woman's fifty-year-old son came to visit and said the words he had never dared to say in over forty years. As a seven-year-old boy playing with matches, he had been responsible for setting the family home on fire and burning it to the ground. The incident had never been mentioned again by anyone in the family. On this day, he finally could say, "I'm so sorry." Just moments later, the woman breathed her last. No one knew whether it was the son's repentance or the mother's opportunity to reassure him that mattered most, but clearly the woman had been waiting for a sense of resolution and closure.

REMEMBRANCES

In my grandmother's generation, it was common to own a small golden locket, which opened to reveal the picture of a loved one tucked inside. The locket was worn as a necklace or broach so that it could be kept close to the heart. Unlike today, when we struggle to organize the thousands of pictures we take, that cherished photograph might have been the only existing likeness of a person. By that single photo, a loved one was remembered and memorialized, and the locket that held it became a prized possession.

After your loved one dies, you may long for a different kind of photo, one that will capture the likeness of your loved one's soul. You may want to have one picture that clearly shows the nature of that person and will become a prized possession for the memories it will harbor. With a relatively small amount of planning, you can create a love "locket" that will become an enduring reminder of your loved one. In the process, you will probably help bring closure to all involved.

One way to create this memento is to make a video capturing your loved one telling a favorite story, a bit of family history, or a joke that has come to be standard fare. Though you may not want to see this right away, in years to come you will be glad to have it. Or you may choose to use audio equipment to record the sound of the person's voice. This may be preferred if the person has gone through a physical transformation that has been difficult to watch. There will come a time when the sound of your loved one's voice will be longed for and having an audio version will be a great comfort.

The written word is another powerful tool for recording the essence of a person. My friend Naomi was widowed at a very young age, when she still had three school-age children at home. Wanting her children to have something lasting and tangible from their father, she asked Israel to write a letter to each child, describing characteristics he saw as special. This became a kind of blessing that he bestowed on each one. Though he wasn't able to finish the written versions himself, he relayed his thoughts to Naomi, who put them to paper. Conversely, each child wrote something special for their father—a letter, a poem, or an essay. These were their tributes to him, and by their choosing were read at his memorial service.

CELEBRATIONS

Illness and death rob us of time with a person we love. One of the ways to take back that time is by making every day special and creating opportunities to celebrate. It is easy to feel that "too much excitement" is negative, but in truth, your loved one will greatly benefit from participating in the making of special memories or having one more reason for family or friends to gather.

Frequently, a person who is dying will set a goal of "making it" to a particular birthday (their own or someone else's), anniversary, graduation, or birth of a child. The person may begin to repeatedly ask how long before that day arrives. For them, time has started to become irrelevant, so it is increasingly difficult to mark the days. If you sense your loved one is looking forward to commemorating a special day, do all you can to make it happen. Talk about the upcoming event, and offer to help select the clothing to be worn. If appropriate, make arrangements for hair to be styled or cut, or for a special shave or nail trimming. Don't let the circumstances deter you! Sometimes, having something to look forward to can make the difference between endless monotony and motivation.

When my mother was too sick to get up anymore but wanted a fresh haircut, her hairdresser came to the house and styled her hair right in bed! It gave Mom just the lift she needed and made her feel beautiful. We capitalized on this by arranging for family portraits to be taken. Little did we know Mom would live only a few more days. Those photographs of my mother are the ones I prize most.

Eleanor, age ninety-three, had been in and out of the hospital for months with a wide array of physical problems. However, she desperately wanted to celebrate her sixty-fifth wedding anniversary, which was on Easter Sunday. Miraculously, she rallied, and her family responded by giving the "newlyweds" a beautiful anniversary celebration. Eleanor died one month later.

My father had been a star athlete in high school. He was a celebrity at his class reunions, which, as years went by, were held with greater frequency. His goal was to attend his sixty-seventh class reunion, so I offered to take him. Though he was in a wheelchair and needed full assistance, he made it! He was able to relive his glory days one more time, but with that goal out of the way, he looked forward to little else. Six months after the reunion he died.

Even if there is not a special day ahead, make celebrations out of ordinary things. Bring flowers, holiday decorations, candles, or music into your loved one's room, and make time for special friends or family members to visit. Commemorate small accomplishments, and go out of the way to create laughter and joy. These times together are special gifts and are the legacy your loved one will leave for others to wear close to their hearts.

CHAPTER 16

Physical Changes

*What if every stroke of pain, or hour of weariness, or
loneliness, or any other trial of flesh or spirit could carry
us a pulse-beat nearer some other life. . . . Would it not be
worthwhile to suffer? Ten thousand times yes.*
—Amy Carmichael

Now that I have seen death several times, I know how it
looks. But when my mother was dying, I had no idea what to
expect. That troubled me. Would I one day walk into her room
only to find her gone without warning? Would I miss my last
chance to comfort her because I didn't understand how little
time she had left? These and a hundred similar questions
plagued me as I saw my mother's health diminishing. Since then,
I have learned to see death coming and am no longer afraid.

KNOWLEDGE EMPOWERS

There are specific physical changes that occur before the
time of death. Knowing these will empower you and make you

more effective in three significant ways. First, this is your last call for taking care of unfinished spiritual business. If you have been waiting for an appropriate time, this is it. You may have been quietly working in the background, serving, gaining trust, and following the lead of the Holy Spirit. Now it is time to come forward and be completely frank with your loved one, for it is truly now or never.

The second way this knowledge will assist you is by letting you know that the physical changes you observe are normal and not to be feared. Knowing what to expect will keep you from panicking or overreacting. If you are prepared, you will be more comfortable and will be able to make the time more meaningful for your loved one, for those around you, and for yourself.

A wonderful booklet on this topic of changes before death is *Gone From My Sight* by Barbara Karnes. The hospital, hospice, or nursing care facility should be able to provide you with a copy, as it is considered the definitive resource for families facing the death of a loved one. Much of the information in this chapter is based on that publication (see the appendix for details).

The third benefit of knowing the visible signs of death is that it will help you see the finish line. Though you love this person and don't want to say good-bye, you may begin to sense that it is time. This is often difficult to admit. Additionally, the constant drain of caring for someone who is terminally ill is mentally, spiritually, and physically exhausting—more than any other thing in this world you will ever do. One thing that makes it so hard is not knowing how long a job it will be. If you knew you had to run ten miles, you could pace yourself and do it. However, if after ten miles, you found out the finish line had been moved, you would be frustrated and irritable. If no one would reveal how far away that line had been moved but insisted you must run indefinitely, your morale would be crushed. Worse yet, you would have no way of gauging whether or not you could finish the race. The death of a loved one is like that. Physical changes that signal the finish line is approaching will make it a little bit easier to keep running.

A DIFFERENT PACE

I mentioned Allison, who was my mother's hospice nurse. Allison was also a great teacher, and she taught me a lot about the dying process. Because of her, I felt prepared for every step of the way.

For quite some time, my mother's condition had been somewhat static. She wasn't losing or gaining ground, just holding her own. From time to time we had a few small scares, but they seemed to work themselves out pretty quickly. During that time, Allison visited once or twice a week, mostly to check vital statistics. She was always upbeat and perky, but insisted I call her if anything should change. Then in one night *everything* changed. When I called Allison to explain my mother's condition, her usually pert voice suddenly had a very serious tone.

I sensed that had we been meeting in person, Allison would have put her hands on my face and turned it to look straight into her eyes. "Listen to me," she began. "This is *very* important. When we start to go downhill, we pick up speed."

It took me a moment to process what she was really saying. We had reached the final downhill slope of my mother's journey. We had been plodding along, sometimes on level ground, sometimes up steeper terrain. We had now crested the last hill, and Allison was warning me to hold on tightly, for we were headed for a wild and rapid descent.

A major health crisis is often a signal that the pace is changing. Or several less significant events in succession can indicate a change is underway. Damage or failure in multiple parts of the body is also a sign that the approach of death is now nearing.

Even when the pace begins to change, you can remain calm and flexible. Remember, you have been on this road for a while, and these changes are a normal part of the dying process. It is not necessary to panic. Instead, find ways to make the person comfortable and feel reminded of your love. If you are caring for your loved one, you might need more help at this time. Be sure to call on those who can assist you, such as hospital or hospice nurses, professional home health workers, or a friend or relative who has indicated a willingness to help.

LEAVING THIS LIFE

The one you love is on a journey headed somewhere far away from here. Because of this, it will be necessary for the person to leave the life he or she has known. Though you have walked alongside on that journey, *you* will remain here, and that person will continue on without you. In preparation for this, distance will develop between that person and the world, including all those who will be left behind.

As time goes on, this distance becomes more obvious. The physical world doesn't seem to matter as much, while the spiritual world becomes more real. You might wonder if your loved one is depressed or brooding, and may be tempted to suggest ways to cheer up or become engaged in activities. This is your attempt to hold on, and a way of trying to keep things as normal as possible. But remember, this distance is necessary and is part of the dying process. As I explained in chapter 14, this is a time when the Holy Spirit may be working in your loved one's heart, so be sensitive to this and don't interfere in any way with what He is doing. You will have a natural tendency to want everything to remain the way it has always been and might find yourself hanging onto routines that no longer matter. Your loved one may now begin to think more about what will happen after death, and will begin preparing for that process. Be ready to answer questions if they arise.

As your loved one begins to feel more distance from this world, you will begin to notice little changes that will communicate this to you. Things that once brought a great deal of pleasure, such as food, visits, grooming, music, or nature, may now be of little importance. If these were once welcomed, they may now be refused. There may be a sudden interest in giving things away, planning a memorial service, or taking care of unfinished business. The person may sleep more than ever before, and seem withdrawn even when awake. These are all part of the distancing process.

The distancing process may take place anywhere from a few months before death up until very close to the time of death.

Sleep

Sleep will begin to take up more and more time, and eventually, there may be only a few moments in the day when the person is awake. Those moments may come at the least welcomed times (such as the middle of the night), for the person's schedule begins to take on a life of its own, no longer ordered by the usual patterns of night and day. At first, sleep is lighter, and the person can be roused by the sound of a familiar voice. Eventually, the slumber deepens, and the person may no longer awaken, but the person is still keenly aware of others in the room. Your voice and touch can offer a great deal of comfort, so speak to the person the way you normally would. Your voice is heard, even when you do not get a response. It may seem awkward in the beginning to speak to the person without a response, but after you do it a few times, it becomes much easier and begins to feel natural.

During this time of increased sleep, it is common to observe jerking or agitated movements that seem to grasp or pick at the air or bedclothes. These movements do not necessarily mean something is wrong. Check to make sure nothing is binding the hands or arms, and offer reassurance with your touch or voice.

Dreams also are vivid and seem to have great significance during this time. The person may talk about having seen Jesus, God, heaven, or deceased loved ones. This is a frequent, almost universal experience, probably due to the fact that the veil between the spiritual realm and the earthly realm is becoming more transparent. Your loved one can now see things that have previously remained invisible. Your first impulse may be to correct your loved one, saying things like, "No, Grandpa isn't here." It is much more interesting, however, to ask questions. You may be surprised at what you learn!

Even after your loved one has begun to sleep most of the time, there are many meaningful and creative ways for you to offer spiritual comfort. If it seems natural to do so, and if there are no facial expressions indicating this is not welcome, you may want to read from the Bible or a devotional book, or sing, pray, or play quiet music. All of these can soothe your loved one on a spiritual level. However, be sensitive, and watch for facial responses. If these activities seem to cause agitation, do not insist on them.

Changes in sleep can be seen throughout the time of illness. However, a few weeks before death, the increase in the amount of sleep is usually very dramatic. The last few days of a person's life may be entirely consumed with sleep.

Appetite

As a person's body begins the process of shutting down, food is not important anymore. Your loved one will become less hungry, indicating nothing tastes good, or may develop difficulty in swallowing. From then on, your loved one will eat less and less.

This change is necessary, but it goes against our natural inclinations. You may believe the person *must* eat in order to stay strong and feel upset if the person does not want to or does not seem able to eat. You may worry the person will starve to death. The truth is, your loved one is already dying, and that is precisely why the appetite is shutting down.

It is helpful for you to think about food as now providing pleasure rather than nutrition. Offer foods that are extremely flavorful and that can remain in the mouth without a lot of chewing. Cool or juicy foods are often preferred. Items such as ice cream, yogurt, Popsicles, sorbet, pudding, Jell-O, applesauce, and soft fruits (grapes, melons, peaches, tropical fruits) are good choices. If your loved one requests or can be coaxed into eating a favorite food (my mom always wanted waffles!), be satisfied with just one or two bites if that is all the person can manage. Also be sure your loved one sits up to eat or drink so as to avoid choking.

If you have a blender, fruit smoothies or slushy beverages in any flavor can be made, and are often enjoyable. If desired, protein powder may be added to boost nutrition. Even blending prepackaged meal replacement drinks (such as Ensure) with ice and/or fruit will make a delicious and nutritional shake that is more appealing than a canned beverage. Your goal is to make food pleasant and safe for your loved one to consume. The creative use of a blender may assist in this process.

If your loved one wears dentures, they may become ill-fitting if a great deal of weight has been lost. In this case, the blender may be used to soften foods so they can be more easily consumed. All hospices have nutritionists who can make appropriate suggestions, so be sure to utilize their services.

If your loved one is diabetic, monitor blood sugar levels until the doctor tells you it no longer matters. At that time, you will probably be released to offer foods that are normally prohibited. However, it is extremely dangerous to do this without doctor approval.

Changes in appetite may begin several months before death. Gradually the appetite decreases. Days or even weeks before death, food and liquids may be refused.

Energy

As your loved one draws closer to death, there may be a visible disorientation to surroundings and to time. You may also notice a decreased response to sights, sounds, or even touch. Even when awake, your loved one may seem to have no energy at all to interact or to focus on things of this world. Then, suddenly, there may be an unexplained burst of energy. Your loved one may ask to sit up, move about, make a phone call, write a letter, or eat a meal. In extreme cases, there may be urgency to take an outing or visit a favorite place or person. This resurgence of strength may be very short-lived, such as a few hours. Or it may last for a week or even longer. These bursts of energy are almost always followed by a pronounced rapid decline.

A burst of energy may occur a few months before the person dies,

and last for several weeks, or may occur only days or hours before
death and be very short in duration.

Skin

A number of changes in the skin can be seen as the body
starts to shut down. Your loved one may feel clammy or dewy,
or perspire so profusely that the bedclothes and linens must be
changed frequently. The body temperature may fluctuate drastically, with a low-grade or even very high fever alternating spo-
radically with periods during which the skin is extremely cold to
the touch.

The coloring of the skin may appear flushed during times of
fever, or may appear gray or bluish. Some people also take on a
yellow or sallow appearance. As circulation slows, the fingernails
and toenails may turn blue or perhaps an icy-white color. Mot-
tling or blotchy patches may begin to appear and can vary from
light red all the way to dark purplish blue. They are most likely
to appear on the hands, feet, legs, undersides of arms, or on the
abdomen, back, or buttocks.

As circulation decreases, the legs, feet, and hands may
become swollen, and skin in these areas will appear very tight.
The skin may even appear to seep liquid, and be wet to the
touch. Your loved one may derive comfort from having these
areas massaged, but be gentle to avoid causing pain.

As the body seeks to eliminate accumulated toxins, the skin
and/or breath may exude an unusual odor. It may not be immediately noticeable, but this odor is a distinct indication that the
dying process has begun. This change usually occurs no more
than a week or two before death.

Closer to the time of death, the skin may become very
drawn-out looking, as though it is hanging loose on the bones.
Or if swelling is present, the skin will seem stretched taut over
the bones. The face especially can seem distorted as former mus-
cle tone disappears.

Just a few days before death, the tongue becomes very dry
and red. It will pull back in the mouth and appear smaller than

normal. As the person breathes, the tongue retracts backward, and may appear tense. This often is accompanied by changes in breathing patterns.

Changes in skin take place a few weeks to a few days before death.

Circulation and Blood Pressure

The blood pressure may become erratic, vacillating from alarmingly high to dangerously low within a relatively short time. The pulse may also vary from the normal rate of eighty up to as high as one hundred fifty beats per minute, or down to no detectable pulse.

If the person is still alert, these drastic changes in the circulatory system can cause changes in disposition. Angry outbursts may result, even if the person is not usually prone to this. It is important to understand these mood alterations are the result of physical changes, and are not a reflection on the relationships that are affected. Try not to take angry words personally. Speak to the person calmly, and do not respond with the same emotion he or she is displaying. This will help the person relax until the blood pressure stabilizes.

Erratic changes in blood pressure can take place at any time, but are common during the last week or days before death.

Body Systems

As the body weakens, it begins to shut down various functions that are no longer needed. Digestion and elimination are the most notably affected (see the previous section on appetite).

The body sometimes begins to eliminate waste more profusely in preparation for death. Both the bowels and the bladder may, over a stretch of several days, completely void. This can be followed by a near cessation of output.

If the heart is not able to properly pump fluids through the body (congestive heart failure), there may be an accumulation of liquids. This can express itself either in swelling (edema), particularly of the extremities, or in an accumulation of fluid in the lungs. If the latter occurs, there may be an accumulation of mucus, which should be suctioned so the person can breathe more easily. If your loved one is hospitalized, medical personnel will attend to this need some of the time, but you can keep your loved one more comfortable if you perform this duty as frequently as is needed. If your loved one is at home, you can request special equipment and/or medication that will assist in this process of clearing liquid from the lungs. Positioning your loved one on the side will also allow the lungs to release liquid and will make breathing easier.

As body systems shut down, you may see shaking or trembling movements. This can be light and occur only in the extremities, or the whole body may shake violently or seem to have a seizure. If this happens, it can be extremely disconcerting to watch. However, your loved one is not experiencing pain while this is taking place. The effects of these movements can be lessened by surrounding the body with a hug and gently holding your loved one until the shaking stops. Speak to your loved one during this time and offer verbal reminders of your love and presence.

When body systems begin to shut down, death is very near. It is best to continue speaking to, praying over, and touching the person while this is taking place, as these will be your final moments together.

Eyes

During regular sleep the eyes of a person are closed, but when a person is dying, the eyes may remain either partially or completely open and appear to stare. Blinking slows and diminishes, and the eyes may become glassy and unable to track or focus. Often the eyes remain open in this manner all the way to the point of death.

It will seem strange to see your loved one's eyes stare in this manner. Though you search the eyes to learn what they are trying to communicate, they will remain fixed and unresponsive. This signals that the crossing over process has already begun.

Your loved one may seem to see something in the distance or may reach out toward someone or something that you cannot see. It is not likely that your loved one will look at you anymore. Now you must rely on your own voice and touch for communication with your loved one. *When the eyes become glassy and fixed, death is very close—usually within hours.*

Hearing and Touch

Hearing and touch are the last remaining connections you will have with your loved one. Hearing normally remains completely intact until the very end, so assume that the person can hear *everything* that is being said. Your loved one will remain aware of your presence because of the sound of your voice and the stroke of your hand, and will be greatly comforted by these. Continue speaking to the person just as you normally would. Pray. Sing. Quote appropriate Bible verses. Say all the words that are on your heart, and trust they are being heard.

Even those who have experienced hearing impairment seem to be extremely sensitive to sound as death approaches. As you speak words of love and comfort, you may want to use a soft voice or even a whisper.

Breathing

Your loved one's breathing will change as the time of death approaches. At times the breath rate will be drastically slow, with breaths so far apart you wonder if breathing has completely stopped. Then breathing may speed up unexpectedly for any given amount of time and later slow down again. Generally while the breathing is still quiet and gentle, death is not imminent.

Hours before death, the breathing may become more gasping and increasingly labored. Frequently, a low throaty gurgling or "rattling" sound accompanies the breath, especially when liquid is present in the lungs. The lips may pucker during inhalation and seem to puff or sip in the air, resembling the puffing and blowing associated with smoking a cigarette. Or the entire lower jaw may drop with each breath. Breathing will no longer look normal but will appear as though air is moving in and out of the body much like a fireplace bellows. Each breath will seem mechanical and unnatural, and the body will almost seem empty, except for the air that is going in and out.

The sound of the air entering and leaving the mouth and lungs may be very raspy during this time. The body may need to heave slightly to help with the effort of taking in the air. When this type of breathing is observed, your loved one is very near the end, and everyone who wishes to be present must come immediately.

The breaths will gradually come farther and farther apart. Breathing may completely stop, and then after several seconds begin again. Eventually, one breath is different from all the others, for it is the very last the person will breathe on this earth. At that moment the person has left this world and entered another realm.

Gone From My Sight

I am standing upon the seashore. A ship at my side spreads her white sail to the morning breeze and starts for the blue ocean. She is an object of beauty and strength. I stand and watch her until at length she hangs like a speck of white cloud just where the sea and sky come to mingle with each other.

Then someone at my side says: "There, she is gone!"

"Gone where?"

Gone from my sight. That is all. She is just as large in mast and hull and spar as she was when she left my side and she is just as able to bear her load of living freight to her destined port.

Her diminished size is in me, not in her.

And just at the moment when someone at my side says: "There, she is gone!" there are other eyes watching her coming, and other voices ready to take up the glad shout: "Here she comes!"

And that is dying.

—Henry Van Dyke (b.1852)

We know that as long as we are at home in this body we are away from the Lord's home. . . . We are full of courage, and would much prefer to leave our home in this body and be at home with the Lord.

—2 CORINTHIANS 5:6, 8 TEV

CHAPTER 17

The Home Going

*But they were looking for a better place, a heavenly
homeland. That is why God is not ashamed to be called
their God, for He has prepared a heavenly city for them.*
—HEBREWS 11:16 NLT

One of the most amazing places in this world is Yosemite
National Park. Monolithic granite walls rise thousands of feet out
of the valley floor, their sharp edges in stark contrast to the
graceful dogwood trees that hover at their feet. Waterfalls
abound, performing a constant, cascading symphony for the eyes
and ears. The silhouettes are wild, extreme, and not what anyone, having never been there, could imagine or expect. Everything Yosemite is extreme and unforgettable.

The hiking in Yosemite is magnificent, like nowhere else. It's
possible to gain over three thousand feet elevation from the valley floor, leading you into surroundings that are completely different from your starting point. From certain vantage points,
scale is skewed, making enormous rivers and falls appear in min-
iature. Around every bend, the view is more breathtaking than

the last. Some of the panoramas are so overwhelming, they bring tears immediately to the eyes. The trails are often ruthless and exhausting, but the rewards are well worth the effort. Visiting Yosemite is a soul-stirring event.

This homeward bound trail you are on is similar. You are standing with someone you love on the breathtaking precipice between this world and the next. The trail has been strenuous, but hopefully you have witnessed the glorious hand of God along the way. Perhaps you have arrived here at the end of the path with an overwhelming sense of the miraculous and the satisfied feeling that it has been worthwhile.

You have done all you could to provide safe passage on this journey. Together you have traveled through the steep ascents into the mountains and have looked down into the valley to see your past life from another perspective. You have been a guide, leading your loved one onto the most reliable path. Now the descent back down into the valley floor has begun. The speed has increased, and soon you will be at the edge of heaven's portal where your loved one will take a few steps farther without you. Then you will continue on another route.

Like any journey, this one has had inherent risks. You have traveled without guarantee of the outcome and have had to trust the Lord all the way to bring about the changes you have desired to see in your loved one's heart. Even now, there is an air of uncertainty.

I don't know exactly how the end of the journey will look for you or for your loved one. But I do know that God has been with you every step so far, and He will be there every step until the very last one. Because of His covenant with you, and because of His great compassion toward your loved one, He will surely extend every opportunity possible for salvation. Whether you see evidence of conversion or not, you must continue in faith and leave the rest to Him.

He will be our guide even to death.
—Psalm 48:14 NKJV

Walking my mother all the way Home was one of the most profound experiences of my life. Neither of us knew exactly what was ahead, but we sensed the journey would somehow be easier together, so we agreed to walk side by side. Often she led. At other times she needed me to be in front. Through the most difficult terrain, she needed assistance, and at times it seemed I carried her. Most of the time she was happy to have my company, but there were also periods when she was resentful— toward God, and me. These were early on in her illness. Later, when it was clear our time together was ending, she changed. The realization came to her that I had given my time, my love, and my effort—not because of an obligation I felt as her daughter, but because of my heartfelt desire to show her, in the only way I knew how, the love of Jesus Christ. It came to her slowly, but finally she understood.

Her old anger with God was suddenly gone, replaced by a familiarity that is usually reserved for those who have walked with the Lord a long time. She spoke of Him as though she had known Him and lived as a Christian her entire life. In our relationship there were changes, too. She became very loving and tender with me and said things that previously had made her uncomfortable. It was as though the real person inside her finally emerged, as naturally and as easily as can be imagined, as though she had always been that way. Our relationship was suddenly more meaningful to both of us than it had ever been. Within these new parameters, we were able to discuss topics we had never dared broach before.

My mom was agonizing about a granddaughter who had not yet reached her potential. In tears, she shared her concerns and disappointments. I stepped out onto what I thought was extremely thin ice and suggested Mom pray for her and leave her in God's hands for now. I was startled to hear her say, "I *have* been praying for her. I *try* to leave her in God's hands, but it is *so hard.*" For the first time in my life, I was having a conversation with my mother about prayer, as though she were one of the ladies in my Bible study. This wasn't the mother I knew; this was a woman who had been touched by the hand of the Lord.

I believe death is very intimate. Some people, by a sheer act of will, choose who will be with them at that moment. That is what happened with my mother. I had walked with her for most of the journey, and I wanted to be there at the very end. I wanted to offer her whatever comfort I could and didn't want her to die alone. But I had other reasons, too. I wanted to finish what I had begun and know I had given all I could. I yearned to know that I had faithfully accomplished my mission—both for my mother and for my heavenly Father.

You will recall that immediately before my mom's cancer diagnosis, she purchased a little house directly across the street from us. It needed a great deal of work, and we wondered if her time might run out before it was finished. Several family members and the deacons from our church all rolled up their sleeves to help finish the project so Mom could spend the last months of her life there. Amazed by this outpouring of love, she determined to throw a party for all who had helped. It was the last big item on her checklist of things to accomplish, and even as her health declined, she insisted on following through with her plan.

The party was given on a clear, crisp autumn afternoon, the Sunday before Thanksgiving. By then Mom was drifting in and out of consciousness, so close friends and family came into her room to spend time with her. From there she could hear the happy sounds of laughter, of children playing, and of friends and relatives visiting as more than sixty people joined together to honor her.

My husband and I, who work in inner city ministry, had fifty turkey dinners to deliver after the party. This had been arranged for months, and there was no one else to do it. My aunt and uncle stayed with Mom, promising to call if anything changed. When we checked in a few hours later, we were told Mom's skin had suddenly become cold and dewy, and her breathing was very rapid and shallow. We rushed back to the house.

Her eyes were half open, staring into nowhere. "I'm here,

Mom," I quietly said. It was obvious her condition had drastically changed. Her eyes no longer saw me, and her breathing was labored, as though she was trying to take in air that was too heavy for her lungs. I placed my hand in hers, and she gently curled her fingers around mine. I desperately wanted to reach her with my love and comfort, but didn't know how. I stroked her hand for a few moments, and then did the only thing that could communicate my heart to her. I sang.

The words to old hymns came flooding back to me. These were hymns I knew she had heard as a child: "It Is Well With My Soul," "Wonderful Words of Life," "What a Friend We Have in Jesus." The singing seemed to calm her, though I wasn't sure if it was because of my voice, the words, or both. When finally I ran out of hymns, the only appropriate song I could think of was one I learned in college choir. The haunting tune is based on the *New World Symphony* by Dvořák:

> Goin' home, goin' home, I'm just goin' home.
> Quiet like, some still day, I'm a-going home.
> Mother's there, 'spectin' me, Father's waiting too.
> Lots of friends gathered there, all the friends I knew.
> Home, Home, I'm going Home.

As I watched her breathing grow even more labored, I knew we were getting close. My mind retraced the journey we had taken together, noting especially the places when it had seemed impossible to keep going. Her heart had changed so much in these past few months, and I knew that for the first time in her life, she was ready. This, I understood, had resulted from the very struggles her illness had brought us. Now, as I sat beside her, holding her hand and singing softly, I understood I had come as far as I could go. I had walked her all the way to the Gate. Her lips puckered and her frail chest heaved as she drank in one last breath. As I sang the final phrase, she paused for a brief moment, and then went on without me. My mother was now safely Home.

What I witnessed that evening was not what I had expected.

Somehow it seemed much more like a birth than a death. It was as though my mother had waited her whole life for this moment, and her heavenly Father had been waiting for it, too. At last she had become the person He meant for her to be.

It Is Well With My Soul

When peace like a river attendeth my way,
When sorrows like sea billows roll,
Whatever my lot, Thou hast taught me to say,
It is well, it is well with my soul.

My sin—oh, the bliss of this glorious thought!
My sin—not in part but the whole,
Is nailed to His cross and I bear it no more!
Praise the Lord, praise the Lord, O my soul!

And, Lord, haste the day when the faith shall be sight,
The clouds be rolled back as a scroll,
The trump shall resound, and the Lord shall descend!
Even so—it is well with my soul!
　　　—Horatio G. Spafford (b.1828)

CHAPTER 18

Grieving Well

*As I went to my knees with only that thought—
"she's gone"—I sensed the Lord saying to me, "If you
must insist that she is gone, at least finish the thought.
'She has gone—where?'" Ah! The thought was completed
in my mind. "Home," I said. "She has gone home!" . . .
What a difference to know that!*

—RAVI ZACHARIAS

It really isn't possible within the confines of language to describe the experience of watching someone you love die. As my parents each began losing their battles with illness, I knew the inevitable was approaching, inching closer and closer. I had heard and spoken the word *death* all of my life, but not until I saw a breathless face that had been alive just a moment before did I realize how hopelessly inadequate language is to express what happens when someone leaves this world and enters another.

The physical evidence is the easiest component of death to

comprehend, for the body shows clear signs that it has shut down and no one is there anymore. Even so, it is nearly impossible to comprehend that a person whom we loved—perhaps all our life—is now *gone*. Previously, our loved one was defined by the facial characteristics, physical build, and style of movement that combined to represent that person to us. When those things disappear, our mind struggles to make sense of what seems impossible. How can our life go on without this person? Is a person temporary? How can someone who has helped shape our life suddenly vanish into midair? None of it seems to make sense.

While my mother was ill, I was the strong one, the practical one. From the moment of her diagnosis, I had understood she was dying, and had braced myself for it. I watched the signs along the way and knew what was coming. And yet at the moment of her death, I was completely surprised by the enormity of feelings I had and how utterly impossible her death seemed to me. I was there for the last breath, had seen it with my own eyes. And yet it was incomprehensible to me that she was gone. As I sat beside her, still incredulous she was no longer in the room, I sobbed for what must have been the better part of an hour. Even then, I hadn't cried enough tears to express the depth of loss I felt. At last I understood that no one is *ever* fully ready for the death of another. We sense we are made to be eternal, and death disorients us to that truth. Coming to terms with this is called grieving.

GIVE YOURSELF TIME

Grieving is difficult work and takes a great deal of time. Grief has a life of its own and can't be rushed or completed within a convenient or designated period. We must pay homage to grief, and for a time it becomes our master, demanding our service. As time passes it exacts even more from us, but eventually it moves on and we are free.

Grief is complicated by exhaustion. *Every* death is emotionally exhausting, but if you were a primary caregiver, or otherwise closely involved, you may also be physically, mentally, and spiritually exhausted. It will be necessary for you to go through a period of rest and recuperation in order to heal, and this process may take longer than you anticipate. This is partly because grief itself is depleting, so it further diminishes your already weakened resources and slows down the process.

The most accurate description of how I felt after my mother died is battle fatigued. I had been on the front lines of a physical and spiritual war zone, and the relentless fighting had taken its toll. For months I was unable to find energy for even the most mundane tasks and felt distanced from my former life. At times it seemed difficult to connect with people who had not experienced the loss of a close loved one. Even though I felt a deep sense of joy and gratitude for my mother's salvation, I knew this victory had been hard-won. I needed a time of restoration.

When Rita died one year later, the effects were not quite as devastating. This was largely due to the fact that she was not my own mother, so the emotions were not quite as raw. Also my responsibilities were not as great. I helped provide care for six weeks, but I did so as part of a team and never bore the full burden by myself. The lighter load I carried allowed me to come to the finish line with greater reserves, so I was able to bounce back a bit more quickly.

In some ways, my reaction to my father's death was the most surprising. Our relationship had become very sweet during the last few years of his life, but I found myself dealing with fierce anger I thought had long been resolved. Perhaps I was unable to deal with that intense level of emotion while he was alive, or worried that doing so might jeopardize God's work in his life. In any case, after his death I was surprised by the ferocity of my anger toward him. My struggle was short-lived, and I remain grateful that I was able to focus on his needs and not my own during the dying process. But this meant that my grieving also had to incorporate the process of finally laying unresolved issues to rest.

In the space of only twenty-eight months, I lost my mother,

stepmother, my friend Arline, and my father. I learned through this that grief is different each time. However, it also seems to be a cumulative experience, with each death somehow compounding the next. Grief is unpredictable, and neither the depth to which we experience it nor its duration can be controlled. The only way to survive grief and ultimately come to terms with it is to meet it head-on. Recognize the feelings you are having, and give them the honor they deserve. This may mean standing still for longer than you want to, or waiting for something—*anything*—to change. But in the seemingly interminable days that are occupied by the sorrow of death, we ourselves are changed.

FINDING HELP

After your loved one dies, it may be helpful to be around people who have gone through a similar loss. Most hospitals, hospices, and many churches offer bereavement groups. The grief group conducted by our hospice was therapeutic because it connected me to others who had been caregivers. Therefore, we had similar scars. As I watched the others heal, I could see there was a continuum with various gradients of grief. This helped me understand I would eventually leave one phase and move on to the next, an insight that gave me incredible hope. These observations were accurate, and sure enough, there came a time when I was able to work through the paralyzing sadness I initially felt. Being part of a group was therefore extremely beneficial to me.

If you sense you are feeling depressed or "stuck," but are not comfortable in a group setting, consider seeking out an individual who can help you. Speaking to someone who has been through a similar situation may be helpful, but if you find you are not moving forward through grief, even incrementally, you may want to confer with your pastor or even a licensed Christian therapist. The feelings surrounding death are extremely heavy and are not meant to be carried alone.

I began this book by saying how very much I wish we could sit together and have a heart-to-heart chat. I end the same way. If we could be together now, I would look straight into your eyes and tell you how very much I think you have accomplished. I would commend you for the sacrifices you have made and the bravery you have shown. I would cry with you over your loss and over what might have been, but more so, I would celebrate with you the victories and the hope, for these are what will last.

Walking alongside a dying unbeliever is perhaps more difficult and heartrending than any other undertaking in this world. Yet what could be more precious in God's eyes? Out of devotion to Him, you have given a portion of your life to help another person understand His love. The Lord treasures what you have done. You may now be tired, or your heart may be filled with sadness, and this can leave you feeling empty. In time, you will be full again. You might wonder if what you did was enough or feel uncertain about the spiritual outcome for your loved one, especially if you never saw any clear evidence that a conversion took place. If you allow it, thoughts like these will plague you and rob you of the joy that could be yours.

During this time when you are reflecting and grieving, I urge you to leave the results in God's hands. This was His work, not yours. He asked you to join in it with Him for a while, and you did that. But it was never up to you to "save" your loved one, to make changes in his or her heart, or to determine the eternal destination of that person. All these matters belong to your heavenly Father. Your role is not to question what He has done or to second-guess the validity of what you contributed. He was with your loved one when you were not able to be there, and He knows everything that took place. Part of grieving well is relinquishing all this to His care. In the meantime, you must trust that someday He will reveal to you all the secret interactions He had with your loved one and will show you just how important a role you played in His purposes being fulfilled.

Even if you had clear evidence that your loved one made a connection with Jesus before the time of death, you may still have nagging doubts or regrets. This is a natural component of grief. Instead of focusing on any aspect that was left undone or replaying how you might have acted differently, try to constantly revisit the successes and thank God for all He did for your loved one. Be sure to thank Him even for things that remain hidden from you. This is a time to ask the Lord to increase your faith and help you have confidence and assurance that what you hoped for regarding your loved one has actually taken place. As the book of Hebrews reminds us,

> Faith is the confidence that what we hope for will actually happen; it gives us assurance about things we cannot see.
> —HEBREWS 11:1 NLT

Another important aspect of grieving is understanding your need to be replenished. The loss of a loved one is very depleting in itself, but if you were also involved in providing care or emotional support for your loved one or others, you will probably find that your reserves are completely gone. If you have grown accustomed to functioning in an exhausted state, you might not even notice how empty you are. If it has become "normal" to constantly pour yourself out without being filled up again, you may have difficulty receiving sustenance, but it is imperative for you to do so. Now is the time to slow down, nurture yourself, and find restoration.

The practical aspects of this must be customized to fit your personality and needs. You may need to plan a relaxing vacation, give yourself permission to forgo routine obligations, or completely clear your schedule to stay home and sleep, read, or putter. Or, you might find it restorative to devise and tackle an exciting project, learn a new skill, or embark upon an adventure. The important thing is to look inward, assess what you need right now, and find a way to bring it to pass. Balance rest with forward movement so that you don't become inert or paralyzed, because grief, if not monitored, can lead to depression. Make a commitment to give yourself adequate time to fully recuperate and be aware that it will probably take at least one year before you begin to feel grounded again. Each day, take a few moments to reflect upon your sadness and loss, but be sure to also celebrate the victories that were accomplished during your loved one's last days.

It is also appropriate for you to ponder the value Jesus Christ places on the service you have rendered in His name. What you have done is highly prized by Him. You may have set out to affect your loved one's eternal status, but by your obedience, you have also affected your own.

> When the Son of Man comes in His glory, and all the holy angels with Him, then He will sit on the throne of His glory. All the nations will be gathered before Him and He will separate them one from another as a shepherd divides his sheep from the goats. And He will set the sheep on His right hand, but the goats on the left. Then the King will say to those on His right hand, "Come you blessed of My Father, inherit the kingdom prepared for you from the foundation of the world: for I was hungry and you gave Me food; I was thirsty and you gave Me drink; I was a stranger and you took Me in; I was naked and you clothed Me; I was sick and you visited Me; I was in prison and you came to Me."
>
> The righteous will answer Him, saying, "Lord, when did we see You hungry and feed You, or thirsty and give You drink? When did we see You a stranger and take You in, or naked and clothe You? Or when did we see You sick, or in prison, and come to You?" And the King will answer and say to them, "Assuredly, I say to you, inasmuch as you did it to one of the least of these My brethren, you did it to Me."
>
> —MATTHEW 25:31–40 NKJV

The kindness you have poured out and the love you have bestowed have all reflected Jesus Christ to another person. But more than that, they have been evidence to your Savior of your love for Him. You stepped out of your own life for a time and made a commitment to serve another. When you gave a drink to the thirsty, clothed the naked, and visited the sick, you were doing it all as unto the Lord. As you walked alongside the other person, you walked alongside Jesus. Now it is time to sit at His feet, lay down your burdens, and rest. He will turn your tears unto joy.

Then Jesus said, "Come to me, all of you who are weary and carry heavy burdens, and I will give you rest."
—MATTHEW 11:28 NLT

Well done, good and faithful servant; you were faithful. . . . Enter into the joy of your Lord.
—MATTHEW 25:21 NKJV

Appendix

RESOURCES

This list of resources includes agencies, Web sites, and books.

- **ADVANCE DIRECTIVES**
  Caring Connections
  800-658-8898   *www.caringinfo.org*
  Provides an online form for advance directives

- **AGING**
  Administration on Aging (AOA)
  Washington, D.C.
  202-619-0724 (helpline)   *www.aoa.gov*
  National Council on the Aging (NCOA)
  Washington, D.C.
  202-479-1200   *www.ncoa.org*
  Focus on the Family's *Complete Guide to Caring for Aging Loved Ones*
      (Tyndale, 2002).

- **ALS (LOU GEHRIG'S) DISEASE**
  ALS Association
  800-782-4747   *www.alsa.org*

- **ALZHEIMER'S DISEASE**
  Alzheimer's Association
  800-272-3900 (24-hour helpline)   *www.alz.org*

- **BOUNDARIES**
  Henry Cloud and John Townsend. *Boundaries: When to Say Yes, When to Say No, to Take Control of Your Life* (Zondervan, 1992).

- **BRAIN DISEASES**
  National Brain Tumor Foundation
  800-934-CURE   *www.nbtf.org*
  Brain Connections Online
  Links to organizations that provide information on brain disorders
  www.massgeneral.org/neurology/pages/brainconnections.htm

- **CANCER**
  American Cancer Society (ACS)
  800-ACS-2345   *www.cancer.org*
  Canadian Cancer Society
  888-939-3333   *www.cancer.ca*
  David Drum. *Making the Chemotherapy Decision* (Lowell House, 2000).
  William A. Fintel, MD, and Gerald R. McDermott, PhD. *Dear God, It's Cancer: A Medical and Spiritual Guide for Patients and Their Families* (Word, 1993, 1997).
  Leukemia and Lymphoma Society of America
  800-955-4572   *www.leukemia.org*
  National Cancer Institute—Cancer Information Service
  800-4CANCER   *www.cancer.gov*

- **CAREGIVING**
  Christian Caregivers
  www.christiancaregivers.org
  Family Caregiver Alliance/National Center on Caregiving
  800-445-8106   *www.caregiver.org*

- **DEVOTIONALS**
  Henry and Richard Blackaby. *Experiencing God Day by Day* (Broadman, 1998).
  Amy Carmichael. *Gold by Moonlight: Sensitive Lessons From a Walk With Pain* (Christian Literature Crusade, reprinted 2000).
  Elisabeth Elliot. *A Path Through Suffering: Discovering the Relationship Between God's Mercy and Our Pain* (Vine Books, 1992).
  Liz Curtis Higgs. *Embrace Grace* (Waterbrook, 2006). Appropriate for a brand-new believer.

- **DIABETES**
  American Diabetes Association
  800-DIABETES　　*www.diabetes.org*
- **DIGESTIVE DISORDERS**
  American Liver Foundation
  800-GOLIVER　　*www.liverfoundation.org*
  National Institute of Diabetes and Digestive and Kidney Disorders
  www.2.niddk.nih.gov
- **DYING PROCESS**
  Barbara Karnes. *Gone From My Sight: The Dying Experience* (Barbara Karnes Books). This booklet is available from doctors or hospice centers, and may be purchased by contacting:
  360-828-7132　　*www.bkbooks.com*
- **FUNERAL PLANNING**
  www.funeralplan.com
  Everything you need to know about planning a funeral, including a free online or printable funeral planning guide.
- **GRIEF**
  Gerald L. Sittser. *A Grace Disguised: How the Soul Grows Through Loss* (Zondervan, 2005).
- **HEART DISEASE**
  American Heart Association (AHA)
  800-AHAUSA1　　*www.americanheart.org*
- **HOME HEALTH CARE**
  National Association for Home Care and Hospice (NAHC)
  202-547-7424　　*www.nahc.org*
- **HOSPICE**
  Caring Connections
  800-658-8898 (helpline)　　*www.caringinfo.org*
  Hospice Foundation of America (HFA)
  800-854-3402　　*www.hospicefoundation.org*
- **HUNTINGTON'S DISEASE**
  Huntington's Disease Society of America
  800-345-HDSA　　*www.hdsa.org*
- **KIDNEY DISEASE**
  National Kidney Foundation
  800-622-9010　　*www.kidney.org*

- *LEGAL ISSUES*
  Christian Legal Society
  703-642-1070   *www.clsnet.org*

- *LEUKEMIA/LYMPHOMA*
  Leukemia and Lymphoma Society of America
  800-955-4572   *www.leukemia.org*

- *LIVER DISEASE*
  American Liver Foundation
  800-GOLIVER   *www.liverfoundation.org*

- *MEDICARE*
  Centers for Medicare and Medicaid Services
  800-MEDICARE   *www.medicare.gov*

- *MULTIPLE SCLEROSIS*
  Multiple Sclerosis Association of America
  800-532-7667 (helpline)   *www.msaa.com*

- *PARKINSON'S DISEASE*
  Parkinson's Disease Foundation
  800-457-6676   *www.pdf.org*

- *PERSONALITIES*
  Florence Littauer. *Personality Plus* (Revell, 1992).

- *STROKE*
  American Stroke Association
  888-549-1776   *www.americanstroke.org*

SCRIPTURE READINGS

- *DEATH*

Psalm 23	Psalm 73:25–28
Psalm 48:14	

- *FORGIVENESS*

Human	*God's*
Matthew 6:14	Psalm 103:8–12
Mark 11:25	Ephesians 1:7
Luke 17:4	1 John 1:9
Ephesians 4:32	
Colossians 3:13	

- **HEAVEN**

  John 14:1–7   Revelation 22:3–4
  Revelation 21:3–4   Revelation 22:17
  Revelation 21:10–23

- **HOPE**

  Psalm 30:1–5   Isaiah 46:4
  Psalm 126:5–6

- **RESURRECTION**

  John 11:25–26   1 Corinthians 15:13–14, 20–22, 54–57

- **SICKNESS**

  Psalm 78:38–39   Psalm 103:13–17

- **SUFFERING**

  Isaiah 53:4   2 Corinthians 4:8–18

MELODY ROSSI, a trained opera singer, has performed with numerous opera companies in venues ranging from the Kennedy Center in Washington, D.C., to the Vatican in Rome. During her singing career she was a regular soloist at the Crystal Cathedral in Garden Grove, California. In 1994, Melody suffered a surgical error that nearly took her life. Her long recovery became a pivotal point in her Christian walk and gave her deep compassion for those suffering from serious illness. After her recovery Melody taught in inner city schools, where she began to see the tremendous needs of urban adolescents and teens. Subsequently she founded Cloud and Fire Ministries, an organization that evangelizes, disciples, and educates at-risk youth. Her writing has appeared in several publications. Melody and her husband live in Granada Hills, California.

This page is a continuation of the copyright page.